Gamestorming

A Playbook for Innovators, Rulebreakers, and Changemakers

Dave Gray, Sunni Brown, and James Macanufo

O'REILLY®

Beijing · Cambridge · Farnham · Köln · Sebastopol · Tokyo

Gamestorming

by Dave Gray, Sunni Brown, and James Macanufo

Published by O'Reilly Media, Inc., 1005 Gravenstein Highway North, Sebastopol, CA 95472.

O'Reilly books may be purchased for educational, business, or sales promotional use. Online editions are also available for most titles (*http://my.safaribooksonline.com*). For more information, contact our corporate/institutional sales department: (800) 998-9938 or *corporate@oreilly.com*.

Editor: Colleen Wheeler

Production Editor: Rachel Monaghan

Copyeditor: Audrey Doyle

Indexer: Fred Brown

Production Services: Octal Publishing, Inc.

Compositor: Nate McDermott

Cover Designer: Mark Paglietti

Interior Designer: Edie Freedman

Illustrators: Dave Gray and Sunni Brown

Printing History:

July 2010: First Edition.

ISBN: 978-0-596-80417-6

[LSI]   [2010-12-17]

To Michael Doyle, my friend and mentor

—Dave Gray

To my mother, who showed all of us the meaning of unconditional love

—Sunni Brown

To Drew Crowley, who is good at it

—James Macanufo

Contents

CHAPTER 6

Games for Exploring

CHAPTER 8

Putting Gamestorming to Work. **253**

Foreword

In the early 1960s, the celebrated children's author Peggy Parrish introduced us to Amelia Bedelia, an overly literal housekeeper. Among other things, Amelia makes a sponge cake with real sponges, replants weeds when told to "weed the garden", and hits the road with a stick when she's told that the family is going to "hit the road" when leaving for a camping trip. My children squeal with laughter when they read about her comical adventures.

I often find myself laughing along with my children, until I think of the Amelia Bedelias I've met at work. Suddenly, the mistakes that people make while trying to perform their jobs aren't so funny. Mistakes that stem from a lack of clarity about the goals and objectives of a project or the failure to consider the ramifications of making a process change in a complex system. Mistakes created from teams who haven't given themselves the freedom to explore alternatives, or from teams who haven't invested the time to choose thoughtfully from the alternatives they've invented or discovered.

Although the loss of productivity caused by these kinds of mistakes is considerable, these mistakes result in more than that. They generate frustration among the team as work must be redone. They result in unnecessary meetings, because once the mistakes are realized, yet *another* meeting must be called to figure out what to do. The mistakes clog up our email inboxes, because instead of being comfortable in knowing whom I must email about what, I instead just *cc:* or, even more insidiously, *bcc:*, everyone.

These mistakes can be prevented through the use of the games described in this book.

Yes, games.

As Dave, Sunni, and James so thoughtfully explain, serious games help organizations solve complex problems through collaborative play. Drawing from their rich and varied experiences and backing it up with theory, Dave, Sunni, and James start with an overview of why these games help organizations become markedly more effective. Armed with this understanding, they then share with us a broad catalog of games that teams can use to solve a variety of complex problems.

As a designer of such games, I am especially impressed that Dave, Sunni, and James have included a wide variety of games, drawn from their experience and the collected experience of many others in our field. The result is that they have written a "Monday Morning Ready" book: you can read this enjoyable book in a single weekend and put the ideas to work when you start work on Monday morning.

Keep your copy of this book handy, though. While you'll likely start with just one or two of the games included here, chances are good that you're going to quickly return to this book, or the website *www.gogamestorm.com*, to see what new games Dave, Sunni, and James (with the help of their dedicated community) have found to help you realize your goals.

—Luke Hohmann
Founder and CEO
The Innovation Games® Company

Preface

IN 1807, THE GRIMM BROTHERS BEGAN COLLECTING FOLK TALES that had, up until that point, never been written down. In 1812, they published a collection of 86 tales under the title *Children's and Household Stories*. By the seventh edition, the last published in their lifetime, the collection had grown to 211 tales. If not for the work of the brothers Grimm, we might never have heard such stories as Rumpelstiltskin, Snow White, Sleeping Beauty, Rapunzel, Cinderella, Hansel and Gretel, Little Red Riding Hood, and the Frog Prince.

Jacob and Wilhelm Grimm were motivated by a few things: as philologists, they wanted to understand the linguistic elements of the stories and their sources; as historians, they wanted to record the stories as they were told in households; as storytellers, they wanted to entertain, and as Germans (there was no single German state at the time) they were interested in understanding and developing a sense of common identity among German-speaking peoples.

A few years ago, the co-authors of this book embarked on a similar project: our goal was to identify a set of emerging methods and approaches to work that have been germinating since the 1970s and are deeply intertwined with the burgeoning Information Age.

Since the invention of the computer chip, we have been moving from an industrial to a post-industrial economy, where the nature of work is changing. In an industrial society, workers are expected to fit standardized job descriptions and perform their duties according to clear policies, procedures, and prescriptions. Knowledge work is fundamentally different: workers are expected not so much to perform standard roles but to generate creative, innovative results that surprise and delight customers and colleagues. They are expected not only to perform a function but to design new and better products and services, and even to provide dramatic, breakthrough results.

Creativity and invention have long been seen as a "black box." As businesspeople, we don't typically try to understand this process. We fully expect that when designers, inventors, and other creative people go into a room with a goal, they will come out with more or less creative discoveries and results. Although when we watch them at work, we can observe some combination of sketching, animated conversations, messy desks, and drinking, the fundamental nature of what happens in that room remains mostly a mystery.

It's easy to leave creativity to the creative types, and say to yourself, "I'm just not a creative person." The fact is that in a complex, dynamic, competitive knowledge economy, it's no longer acceptable to take this position. If you are a knowledge worker, you must become, to some degree, creative.

That may sound a bit scary, but the fact is that successful creative people tend to employ simple strategies and practices to get where they want to go. It's not so much that they employ a consistent, repeatable process that leads to consistent creative results. It's more like a workshop with a set of tools and strategies for examining things deeply, for exploring new ideas, and for performing experiments and testing hypotheses, to generate new and surprising insights and results.

So my co-authors and I set out, much like the brothers Grimm, to collect the best of these practices wherever we could find them, with a special focus on Silicon Valley, innovative companies, and the information revolution.

Many of these practices emerged from a kind of "Silicon soup"—the deeply interconnected network of Silicon Valley, where ideas and people cross-pollinate like bees in a single massive hive. The practices live in a mostly oral culture, passed along from person to person by word of mouth. For example, a consultant uses an approach with a client, and the client begins to employ that approach internally. Over time, as more people employ a method, it evolves into something quite different, and over time the source of the original idea or approach may be lost. Sometimes methods are written down and sometimes, like folk tales, they exist in many different versions in many places.

We chose to call the book *Gamestorming* because it seemed to come closer to describing the phenomenon than anything else we could think of. In the front section, we've done our best to provide a sense of the underlying mechanics or architecture of the games we describe, as well as some design principles that may be helpful as you begin to try out the practices for yourself.

It is our hope to create a volume that will be of use to the novice and the experienced practitioner alike. If you're a novice, we hope you'll find a whole new world of ideas for how to approach various challenges in your work. For the experienced practitioner, we hope you'll find some good ideas and a few things that are "new to you."

Our goal with this collection was to find the best of these tools and practices and bring them together into a single volume.

One of our biggest challenges has been establishing the provenance of each game and sourcing it appropriately. At times, it can be very difficult to determine who first designed a tool or where it was first used. We have done our best to determine the source of each game and have made notes where possible, while at the same time doing our best not to distract from the primary content. Often it seemed that we found ourselves looking at a series of Russian dolls—whenever we identified the source of a game, it seemed that it may have been derived from another, earlier source, and it always seemed that there might be a previous claimant lurking in the wings.

When we use the term "based on," the description is based on some kind of written material where we have identified a source. When we use the term "inspired by," we have identified the premise, idea, or core concept, but the game itself was based on oral histories or our own design. If we were unable to identify a source reliably, we have marked the game source as unknown. If you have ideas about the origins of these games, please share them with us.

In fact, we fully expect that as we engage with a larger community around this project, we will add more games, refine the overall collection, and improve our understanding of the rich history of these games in future editions. We have set up an online forum at *www.gogamestorm.com*, where we'd like to enlist your help. It is our hope that you will contribute games based on your personal knowledge and experience, that you will help us clarify the history of the ideas and practices, and that through your comments you can help us all better understand the complex and fascinating history of games at play in creative work.

—Dave Gray
Saint Louis
June 2010

CHAPTER 1

What Is a Game?

GAMES AND PLAY ARE NOT THE SAME THING.

Imagine a boy playing with a ball. He kicks the ball against a wall, and the ball bounces back to him. He stops the ball with his foot and kicks it again. By engaging in this kind of play, the boy learns to associate certain movements of his body with the movements of the ball in space. We could call this *associative play*.

Now imagine that the boy is waiting for a friend. The friend appears, and the two boys begin to walk down a sidewalk together, kicking the ball back and forth as they go. Now the play has gained a social dimension; one boy's actions suggest a response, and vice versa. You could think of this form of play as a kind of improvised conversation, where the two boys engage each other using the ball as a medium. This kind of play has no clear beginning or end; rather, it flows seamlessly from one state into another. We could call this *streaming play*.

Now imagine that the boys come to a small park, and that they become bored simply kicking the ball back and forth. One boy says to the other, "Let's take turns trying to hit that tree. You have to kick the ball from behind this line." The boy draws a line by dragging his heel through the dirt. "We'll take turns kicking the ball. Each time you hit the tree you get a point. First one to five wins." The other boy agrees and they begin to play. Now the play has become a game; a fundamentally different kind of play.

What makes a game different? We can break down this very simple game into some basic components that separate it from other kinds of play.

> **Game space:** To enter into a game is to enter another kind of space where the rules of ordinary life are temporarily suspended and replaced with the rules of the game. In effect, a game creates an alternative world, a model world. To enter a game space, the players must agree to abide by the rules of that space, and they must enter willingly. It's not a game if people are forced to play. This agreement among the players to temporarily suspend reality creates a safe place where the players can engage in behavior that might be risky, uncomfortable, or even rude in their normal lives. By agreeing to a set of rules (stay behind the line, take turns kicking the ball, etc.), the two boys enter a shared world. Without that agreement, the game would not be possible.

Boundaries: A game has boundaries in time and space. There is a time when a game begins—when the players enter the game space—and a time when they leave the game space, ending the game. The game space can be paused or activated by agreement of the players. We can imagine that the players agree to pause the game for lunch, or so that one of them can go to the bathroom. The game will usually have a spatial boundary, outside of which the rules do not apply. Imagine, for example, that spectators gather to observe the kicking contest. It's easy to see that they could not insert themselves between a player and the tree, or distract the players, without spoiling or at least changing the game.

Rules for interaction: Within the game space, players agree to abide by rules that define the way the game world operates. The game rules define the constraints of the game space, just as physical laws, like gravity, constrain the real world. According to the rules of the game world, a boy could no more kick the ball from the wrong side of the line than he could make a ball fall up. Of course, he could do this, but not without violating the game space—something we call cheating.

Artifacts: Most games employ physical artifacts; objects that hold information about the game, either intrinsically or by virtue of their position. The ball and the tree in our game are such objects. When the ball hits the tree a point is scored. That's information. Artifacts can be used to track progress and to maintain a picture of the game's current state. We can easily imagine, for example, that as each point is scored, the boys place a stone on the ground or make hash marks in the dirt to help them keep track of the score—another kind of information artifact. The players are also artifacts in the sense that their position can hold information about the state of a game. Compare the position of players on a sports field to the pieces on a chessboard.

Goal: Players must have a way to know when the game is over; an end state that they are all striving to attain, that is understood and agreed to by all players. Sometimes a game can be timed, as in many sports, such as football. In our case, a goal is met every time a player hits the tree with the ball, and the game ends when the first player reaches five points.

We can find these familiar elements in any game, whether it is chess, tennis, poker, ring-around-the-rosie, or the games you will find in this book.

The Evolution of the Game World

Every game is a world which evolves in stages, as follows: imagine the world, create the world, open the world, explore the world, and close the world. Here's how it works:

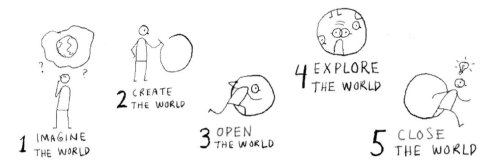

Imagine the world. Before the game can begin you must imagine a possible world; a temporary space, within which players can explore any set of ideas or possibilities.

Create the world. A game world is formed by giving it boundaries, rules, and artifacts. Boundaries are the spatial and temporal boundaries of the world; its beginning and end, and its edges. Rules are the laws that govern the world; artifacts are the things that populate the world.

Open the world. A game world can only be entered by agreement among the players. To agree, they must understand the game's boundaries, rules, artifacts; what they represent, how they operate, and so on.

Explore the world. Goals are the animating force that drives exploration; they provide a necessary tension between the initial condition of the world and some desired state. Goals can be defined in advance or by the players within the context of the game. Once players have entered the world they try to realize their goals within the constraints of the game world's system. They interact with artifacts, test ideas, try out various strategies, and adapt to changing conditions as the game progresses, in their drive to achieve their goals.

Close the world. A game is finished when the game's goals have been met. Although achieving a goal gives the players a sense of gratification and accomplishment, the goal is not really the point of the game so much as a kind of marker to ceremonially close the game space. The point of the game is the play itself, the exploration of an imaginary space that happens during the play, and the insights that come from that exploration.

Imagine the world, create the world, open the world, explore the world, and close the world. The first two stages are the game design, and the remaining three stages are the play.

You can see that a game, once designed, can be played an infinite number of times. So, if you're playing a predesigned game there will be only three stages: open the world, explore the world, and close the world.

Gamestorming is about creating game worlds specifically to explore and examine business challenges, to improve collaboration, and to generate novel insights about the way the world works and what kinds of possibilities we might find there. Game worlds are alternative realities—parallel universes that we can create and explore, limited only by our imagination. A game can be carefully designed in advance or put together in an instant, with found materials. A game can take 15 minutes or several days to complete. The number of possible games, like the number of possible worlds, is infinite. By imagining, creating, and exploring possible worlds, you will open the door to breakthrough thinking and real innovation.

The Game of Business

Let's begin by boiling the "game of business" down to its most basic components.

Business, like many other human activities, is built around goals. Goals are a way we move from A to B; from where we are to where we want to be. A goal sets up a tension between a current state A—an initial condition—and a targeted future state B—the goal. In between A and B is something we can call the challenge space; the ground we need to cover in order to get there.

A
•
Initial
Conditions

CHALLENGE
SPACE

B
•
Target
State
(goal)

In industrial work, we want to manage work for consistent, repeatable, predictable results. Industrial goals are best when they are specific and quantifiable. In such cases, we want to ensure that our goals are as clear and unambiguous as possible. The more specific and measurable the goal is, the better. When we have a clear, precise industrial goal, the best way to address the challenge space is with a business process—a series of steps that, if followed precisely, will create a chain of cause and effect that will lead consistently to the same result.

A
•→•→•→•→•→•→•
B
CLEAR,
UNAMBIGUOUS
GOAL

BUSINESS PROCESS
(A SERIES OF STEPS,
CAUSE AND EFFECT)

But in knowledge work we need to manage for creativity—in effect, we don't want predictability so much as breakthrough ideas, which are inherently unpredictable. In any creative endeavor, the goal is not to incrementally improve on the past but to generate something new.

New, by definition, means "not seen before." So, if a team wants to truly create, there is simply no way to precisely define the goal in advance, because there are too many unknowns. Embarking on this kind of project is akin to a voyage of discovery: like Columbus, you may begin your journey by searching for a route to India, but you might find something like America; completely different, but perhaps more valuable.

Fuzzy Goals

Like Columbus, in order to move toward an uncertain future, you need to set a course. But how do you set a course when the destination is unknown? This is where it becomes necessary to imagine a world; a future world that is different from our own. Somehow we need to imagine a world that we can't really fully conceive yet—a world that we can see only dimly, as if through a fog.

In knowledge work we need our goals to be fuzzy.

Gamestorming is an alternative to the traditional business process. In gamestorming, goals are not precise, and so the way we approach the challenge space cannot be designed in advance, nor can it be fully predicted.

While a business process creates a solid, secure chain of cause and effect, gamestorming creates something different: not a chain, but a framework for exploration, experimentation, and trial and error. The path to the goal is not clear, and the goal may in fact change.

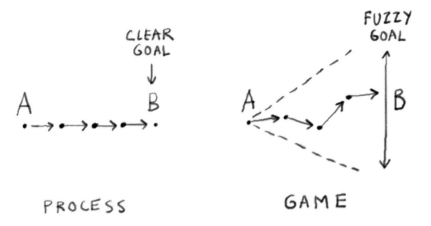

CLEAR
GOAL

FUZZY
GOAL

A   B   A   B

PROCESS   GAME

This is true at both a micro scale and a macro scale. To create a complex industrial product requires the close integration of many processes. When you string a bunch of processes together you will see a branching structure with many dependencies. As long as every step is followed precisely and nothing changes along the way, you will achieve your goal reliably and predictably every time. The management challenge is one of precision, accuracy, and consistency.

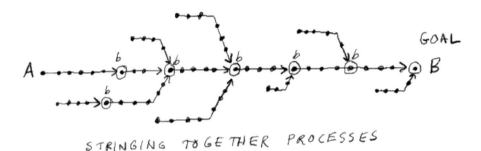

GOAL

A   B

STRINGING TOGETHER PROCESSES

Managing creative work requires a different approach. Because the goal cannot be determined precisely in advance, a project must proceed based on intuition, hypotheses, and guesses. This kind of approach is very familiar in the world of the military, where ambiguous, uncertain, volatile environments are the norm.

We all know that the military uses games and simulations as a way to practice for war. But they also use something called a concept of operations, or CONOPS, to (1) create an overall picture of the system and the goals that they want to achieve, and (2) communicate that picture to the people who will work together to reach those goals. A concept of operations is a way to say, "Given what we know today, here is how we think this system works, and here is how we plan to approach it."

A concept of operations is a way to imagine a world.

This may seem like a big challenge, but think about our two boys playing ball: the world we create does not necessarily need to be complicated to be interesting and to help us move forward. Imagining a world can be as simple or as complex as you want to make it, depending on your goal, your situation, and the time you have available.

Unlike a large and complex process, which must be planned in advance, a concept of operations is under constant revision and adjustment based on what you learn as you go. So, yes, you need to have a goal, but since you really know very little about the challenge space, it's very likely that your goal will change as you try out ideas and learn more about what works and what doesn't.

In gamestorming, games are not links in a chain, so much as battles in a campaign.

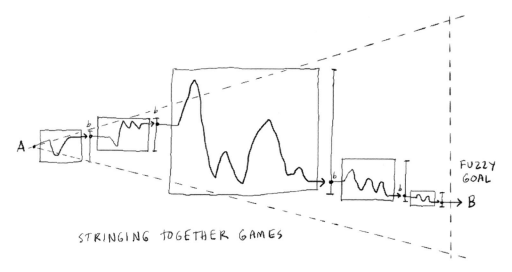

STRINGING TOGETHER GAMES

In a paper titled "Radical innovation: crossing boundaries with interdisciplinary teams," Cambridge researcher Alan Blackwell and colleagues identified fuzzy goals (they called it a pole-star vision) as an essential element of successful innovation. A fuzzy goal is one that "motivates the general direction of the work, without blinding the team to opportunities along the journey." One leader described his approach as "sideways management." Important factors identified by the Cambridge research team include the balance between focus and serendipity, and coordinating team goals and the goals of individual collaborators.

Fuzzy goals straddle the space between two contradictory criteria. At one end of the spectrum is the clear, specific, quantifiable goal, such as 1,000 units or $1,000. At the other end is the goal that is so vague as to be, in practice, impossible to achieve; for example, peace on Earth or a theory of everything. While these kinds of goals may be noble, and even theoretically achievable, they lack sufficient definition to focus the creative activity. Fuzzy goals must give a team a sense of direction and purpose while leaving team members free to follow their intuition.

What is the optimal level of fuzziness? To define a fuzzy goal you need a certain amount of ESP: fuzzy goals are Emotional, Sensory, and Progressive.

Emotional: Fuzzy goals must be aligned with people's passion and energy for the project. It's this passion and energy that gives creative projects their momentum; therefore, fuzzy goals must have a compelling emotional component.

Sensory: The more tangible you can make a goal, the easier it is to share it with others. Sketches and crude physical models help to bring form to ideas that might otherwise be too vague to grasp. You may be able to visualize the goal itself, or you may be able to visualize an effect of the goal, such as a customer experience. Either way, before a goal can be shared it needs to be made explicit in some way.

Progressive: Fuzzy goals are not static; they change over time. This is because, when you begin to move toward a fuzzy goal, you don't know what you don't know. The process of moving toward the goal is also a learning process, sometimes called *successive approximation*. As the team learns, the goals may change, so it's important to stop every once in awhile and look around. Fuzzy goals must be adjusted (and sometimes, completely changed) based on what you learn as you go.

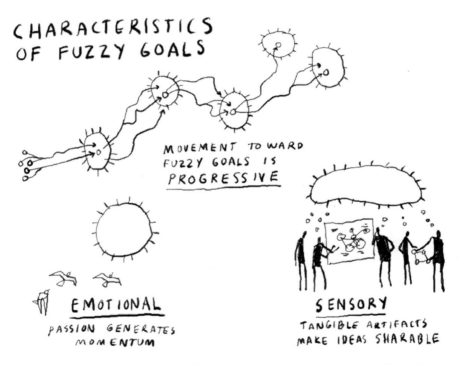

CHARACTERISTICS OF FUZZY GOALS

MOVEMENT TOWARD FUZZY GOALS IS PROGRESSIVE

EMOTIONAL
PASSION GENERATES MOMENTUM

SENSORY
TANGIBLE ARTIFACTS MAKE IDEAS SHARABLE

Innovative teams need to navigate ambiguous, uncertain, and often complex information spaces. What is unknown usually far outweighs what is known. In many ways it's a journey in the fog, where the case studies haven't been written yet, and there are no examples of where it's been done successfully before. Voyages of discovery involve greater risks and more failures along the way than other endeavors. But the rewards are worth it.

Game Design

If you want to get started with gamestorming right away, you can flip to the collection of games that begins with Chapter 5 and start making things happen in your workplace. But if you want to really master gamestorming, you'll need to learn how to design your own games, based on your goals and more specific to what you want to accomplish.

Let's start with this idea. A game has a shape. It looks something like a stubby pencil sharpened at both ends. The goal of the game is to get from A, the initial state, to B, the target state, or goal of the game. In between A and B you have the stubby pencil—that's the shape you need to fill in with your game design.

Target State: To design a game you begin with the end in mind: you need to know the goal of the game. What do you want to have accomplished by the end of the game? What does victory look like? What's the takeaway? That's the outcome of the game, the target state. I like to think of the target state in terms of some tangible thing, which can be anything from a prototype to a project plan or a list of ideas for further exploration. Remember, it helps if a goal is tangible; it gives people something meaningful to shoot for and gives them a sense of accomplishment when they have finished. And when they are done, they'll be able to look at something they created together.

Initial State: We also need to know what the initial state looks like. What do we know now? What don't we know? Who is on the team? What resources do we have available?

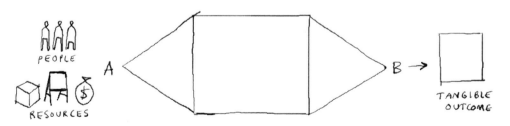

Once we understand the initial and target states as best we can (remember that many goals are fuzzy!), it's time to fill in the shape of the game. A game, like a good movie, unfolds in three acts.

The first act opens the world by setting the stage, introducing the players, and developing the themes, ideas, and information that will populate your world. In the second act, you will explore and experiment with the themes you develop in act one. In the third act, you will come to conclusions, make decisions, and plan for the actions that will serve as the inputs for the next thing that happens, whether it's another game or something else.

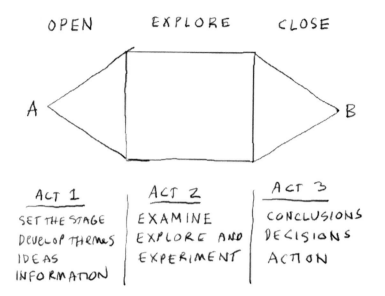

Each of the three stages of the game has a different purpose.

Opening: The first act is the opening act, and it's all about opening—opening people's minds, opening up possibilities. The opening act is about getting the people in the room, the cards on the table, the information and ideas flowing. You can think of the opening as a big bang, an explosion of ideas and opportunities.

The more ideas you can get out in the open, the more you will have to work with in the next stage. The opening is not the time for critical thinking or skepticism; it's the time for blue-sky thinking, brainstorming, energy, and optimism. The keyword for opening is "divergent": you want the widest possible spread of perspectives; you want to populate your world with as many and as diverse a set of ideas as you can.

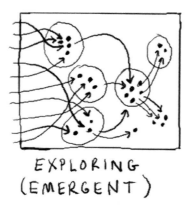

EXPLORING
(EMERGENT)

Exploring: Once you have the energy and the ideas flowing into the room, you need to do some exploration and experimentation. This is where the rubber hits the road, where you look for patterns and analogies, try to see old things in new ways, sift and sort through ideas, build and test things, and so on. The keyword for the exploring stage is "emergent": you want to create the conditions that will allow unexpected, surprising, and delightful things to emerge.

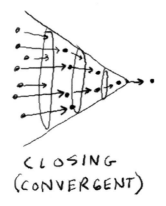

CLOSING
(CONVERGENT)

Closing: In the final act you want to move toward conclusions—toward decisions, actions, and next steps. This is the time to assess ideas, to look at them with a critical or realistic eye. You can't do everything or pursue every opportunity. Which of them are the most promising? Where do you want to invest your time and energy? The keyword for the closing act is "convergent": you want to narrow the field in order to select the most promising things for whatever comes next.

When you are designing an exercise or workshop, you want to think like a composer, orchestrating the activities to achieve the right harmony between creativity, reflection, thinking, energy, and decision making. There is no single right way to design a game. Every company, and every country, has its own unique culture, and every group has its own dynamic. Some need to move faster than others, and some need more time for reflection.

For example, in Finland, long silences where people consider and reflect on a question before answering are not uncommon. This can feel very uncomfortable if you're not accustomed to that culture. You'll need to do your homework and compose a flow that's right for the group you are working with, and the situation you are working on.

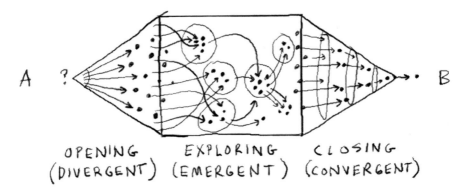

OPENING   EXPLORING   CLOSING
(DIVERGENT)   (EMERGENT)   (CONVERGENT)

Opening, exploring, and closing are the core principles that will help you orchestrate the flow and get the best possible outcomes from any group. A typical daylong workshop may be filled with many games that can be linked to each other in an infinite variety of ways. Games can be played in series, where the outcomes of one game create the initial conditions for the next.

Here's a series where three games are played in a row. Each game has a clear opening, exploration, and closing. The outcome of each game serves as the input for the next. This kind of design is very simple, clear, and easy for everyone in the group to understand.

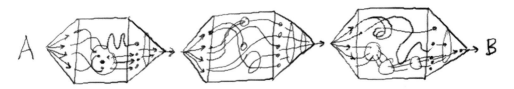

In the next series, three longer, more intensive games are interspersed with two shorter games. The shorter games might give the groups a chance to loosen up a bit between more intensive activities.

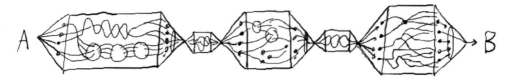

Sometimes, especially with a larger group, it makes sense to pursue multiple goals. A key concept in game design is a variation on opening and closing called break out/report back, where a larger group diverges by breaking out into smaller subgroups, plays a game or two, and converges by reporting back the outcome of their efforts to the larger group. This is a way to keep groups small and dynamic, and also increase the variety of ideas, by playing multiple games in parallel.

People also need time to reflect on ideas. Breakouts (or breaks) can be a good time for this. Break out/report back is a way to balance sharing and reflection and to create quiet time. For example, you can ask people in a group to spend time working on an individual exercise which they can then share with the group.

Here's a series where an initial, opening session reveals three different goals that can be pursued in parallel breakout groups. At the end of the series the three groups' outcomes are shared in a report-back session with the larger group.

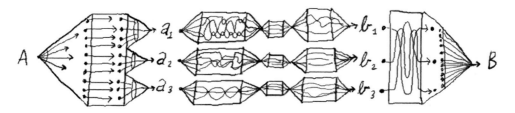

Here's a series where the outcomes of the first game generate inputs for five games, which generate inputs for two games, which generate the input for a single, longer game. This kind of string might indicate a workshop including multiple ideas and agendas that need to be worked on in parallel.

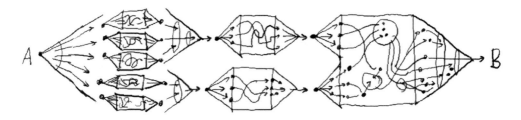

Here's a daylong game where a big chunk of the morning is spent on divergent activities, generating a lot of ideas and information, and the exploration phase is split into two parts, with a break for lunch, followed by an afternoon of convergent activities that flow into a single outcome. The group will lunch together at four tables for informal conversation and reflection on the morning's activities before going into the afternoon session. This kind of design might be appropriate for a group where everyone had some level of interest in every component of the day, and nobody wanted to be left out of any part of the game.

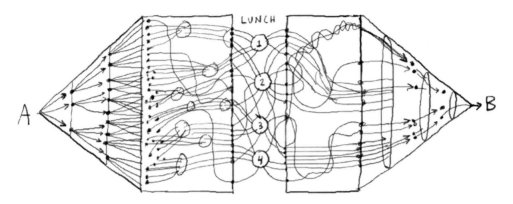

Sometimes you make discoveries while a game is underway that require a change in direction. In the following series, the initial opening and exploration revealed a new goal that the team had not anticipated. The group agreed to break into two subgroups; one group pursued the original goal and the second worked on the new goal.

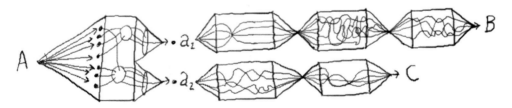

OK, so it's time to compose a game, or maybe a series of games. Where do you begin? What do you compose with? Remember that gamestorming is a way to approach work when you want unpredictable, surprising, or breakthrough results—a method for exploration and discovery.

Think about the people who explored the natural world for a moment: people like Columbus, Lewis and Clark, Ernest Shackleton, and Admiral Byrd. Imagine what it must have felt like to be one of these explorers. You are searching for something that you may not find. You will almost certainly find things you don't expect. You have only a vague idea of what you will encounter along the way, and yet, like a turtle, you must carry everything you need on your back.

CHAPTER 2

10 Essentials for Gamestorming

IN THE 1930s, THE MOUNTAINEERS CLUB DEVELOPED A LIST they called the 10 essentials, for people who want to explore in backcountry or wilderness areas. These are the things you want to be sure you have anytime you go into the backcountry. They include matches, blanket, flashlight, and so on. The point of the 10 essentials is to have a checklist of the items you'll need to be self-sufficient as you explore unknown territory.

We're entering a new age of discovery where we are exploring a world of information. Like the explorers of the past, we often have only a vague sense of what we are looking for and are not sure what we will find when we get there. Based on our collective experience, we have compiled a list of the 10 essentials for gamestorming. It's not an exhaustive list by any means, but rather a solid, dependable, basic toolkit. It's a list of tried-and-true methods: the 20% of the toolkit that you'll use 80% of the time.

These are the methods we employ most often in our work, and they are also the things you will find most useful if you find yourself in a difficult meeting. If you practice and become comfortable with these 10 things, you will be able to work your way through nearly any challenge.

1. Opening and Closing

We've already discussed the importance of opening and closing, but this concept is so important for managing energy and flow that it belongs on the essentials list. Opening and closing is the way you orchestrate your gamestorming activities. Like breathing, it underlies every activity, giving it rhythm and life.

Think about the opening and closing arguments in a court trial. The purpose of the opening is to establish a frame of reference, set the context, and lay out the themes that will be explored in the trial. The closing argument precedes and prepares the way for the jury or judge to make a decision.

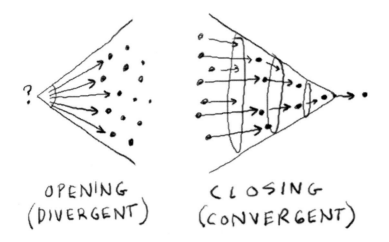

OPENING
(DIVERGENT)

CLOSING
(CONVERGENT)

Opening is just what it sounds like—it's a beginning. To open is to get people thinking and spark their imaginations. To open you need to create a comfortable environment where people feel invited and welcome so that they will open their minds and explore possibilities they may not have considered before. Closing is about bringing things to a conclusion, moving from thinking mode into doing mode. Closing is about making choices and decisions. Break out/report back is a form of opening and closing: you open or break out to find divergent ideas and perspectives, and you close or report back to share ideas and realign with the group.

Here are some risks to be aware of:

Don't open and close at the same time. You can't be creative and critical simultaneously. People's minds just don't work that way. When you are exploring creative possibilities you need to shut down the critical part of your mind, and when you are making difficult choices, you should not try to be creative. Keep them separate and do them in order.

Close everything you open. If you open something you must close it, or you will risk losing the energy of the group. Opening can feel overwhelming. If you open and don't close, people may feel as if you have opened Pandora's box: there are too many opportunities and no plan to tackle them. If people do work in a breakout session, they will be disappointed if they don't have a chance to share it with others and you may miss an important learning opportunity.

Sometimes closing can be as simple as saying, "This thread doesn't seem to be taking us anywhere, so let's not waste anymore time on it."

2. Fire Starting

In knowledge work, fire-starting techniques are the spark that ignites the imagination, a call to adventure. They initiate a quest or search. In the wilderness, the way you start a fire is very important, and in gamestorming the same is true. Start a fire in the wrong way or in the wrong place, and you may soon find that things are out of control—you can have a raging forest fire on your hands. By the way you initiate an inquiry you can inspire the kinds of thought, reflection, emotion, and sensation that are most likely to get you the result that you want.

The most common and powerful fire-starter is the question. A good question is like an arrow you can aim at any challenge. The way you frame a question will lay out a vector, a line of inquiry that points in a certain direction. There are many kinds of questioning techniques and they bear careful study and practice. You can use them to change people's perspectives on a problem, drill down to expose root causes, elevate a conversation to a higher plane, and many other things.

Another common fire-starter is called fill-in-the-blank, in which you craft a short phrase or sentence and ask people to fill in the blank like they would on a test. For example, if you want to explore customer needs, consider how customer needs are typically expressed. A fill-in-the-blank to explore customer needs could be written as "I want _____." (Fill in the blank.)

3. Artifacts

As you begin to collect, sort, and organize information it can quickly become overwhelming. How do you keep track of it all? In archeology, an artifact is anything made or shaped by a human hand—especially when it has archaeological or historical interest. In knowledge work, an artifact is any tangible, portable object that holds information. An artifact can be anything from a piece of paper to a sticky note or index card. Artifacts make it easier to keep track of information by making it a part of the environment.

The pieces in any game, such as cards, counters, and dice, are artifacts. When you do something as simple as moving salt- and peppershakers on a tabletop to tell a story, you are transforming them into knowledge artifacts for the sake of your tale.

The importance of these artifacts as an aid to thinking can easily be illustrated if you imagine yourself playing a game of chess while blindfolded. It's possible to hold the positions of all the pieces in your mind's eye for a time—and most chess masters can do it for an entire game—but it's much easier to have the pieces displayed on a board in front of you. The shape and color of each piece, and its position relative to the board and to the other pieces, contains a rich set of information that can help you make better decisions about the game.

Artifacts are carriers of meaning; just like chess pieces on a board, they make knowledge or information explicit, tangible, portable, and persistent. When you write an idea on a sticky note you are creating an information artifact. When you have created many such artifacts, they can become more or less useful depending on how you distribute them in your environment. The more information you can store in material objects or the environment, the more your players' minds are free to engage with the situation at hand.

4. Node Generation

A node is anything when seen as part of a larger system. As a knowledge explorer, when you create artifacts you will usually be thinking of them as elements in something larger. In the opening stages of any inquiry, the first order of business is to generate as many artifacts—nodes—as possible, so you want to begin from as wide an angle as possible. We call this kind of exercise node generation.

node
generation

One method for generating nodes is called the Post-Up (see a full description in Chapter 4). To post up, you begin with some kind of fire-starter to set the parameters that define your list. To start with a simple example, imagine that you are going shopping and need to create a list of groceries. You could start with a simple question: "What do I need from the store?" Instead of a typical brainstorming session, where people call out ideas and a facilitator makes a list that everyone can see, you ask people to generate their ideas silently, using sticky notes—one idea per note.

the post-up

Doing this accomplishes two goals. First, since it's an opening exercise, you will get a more diverse set of ideas by asking people to generate them silently. Second, by asking people to write each idea on a separate sticky note, you are generating a set of modular, movable artifacts that you will later be able to shuffle, sort, and reorganize.

When people are finished generating ideas, ask them to take turns going up to a flip chart or whiteboard and sharing their ideas with the group, as follows: read each sticky note aloud and place it on the board where everyone can see it. Notice that this Post-Up process is a version of break out/report back. The breakout begins when you ask people to start writing ideas, and the report back ends when everyone has finished sharing ideas and the board is filled with sticky notes.

5. Meaningful Space

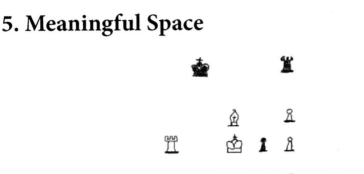

White to mate in 2 moves.

Imagine trying to play chess without a board. A game like chess relies not only on the meaning of the pieces but also on the ever-changing relationships they have to each other in space. The grid of the chessboard creates a meaningful space as cleanly and as surely as the grid on any map. Both the grid and the pieces are integral and essential to the game.

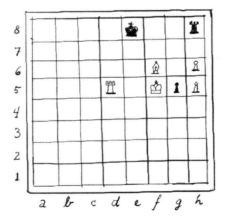

Just like every other game, chess creates a world that players can explore together. The chessboard (meaningful space) creates the boundaries of the world, and the pieces (artifacts) populate the world.

The rules of the game govern what is and isn't possible in the world. Chess players agree to enter the world in order to explore the possible permutations and combinations and try to achieve their goals, which, in the case of chess, are achieved at the expense of the other player. However, in gamestorming, more often the players share a common goal.

For the knowledge explorer, meaningful space can be created anywhere: on a whiteboard, flip chart, or piece of paper; on a tabletop or in a room. It's a way of framing any space to make relationships within it more meaningful. The grid, like the grid of a chessboard, is one of the most common and useful ways to organize space. You can see grids all around you; we use grids for everything from planning cities to managing the numbers in our spreadsheets.

Affinity mapping is a common method that uses meaningful space to sort a large set of nodes into a few common themes. It is a way to rapidly get a group of people aligned about what they are working on together. First, generate a set of nodes using the Post-Up game or some other node-generation method (see Chapter 4).

Next, create a meaningful space by dividing a whiteboard or other visual area into three columns. Ask people to sort the sticky notes into three columns that "feel like they belong together" without trying to name the columns. It's important that they not try to name the columns. Naming the columns too early will force them back into familiar, comfortable patterns. Remember that in creative work we are trying to help people generate and see new patterns. While people are sorting, you may ask them to try to eliminate redundancies by placing similar sticky notes on top of each other. Sometimes the sticky notes don't fit neatly into three columns and you may want to create more columns to accommodate the differences. You should do this sparingly, though, because too many categories will defeat your purpose, which is to find some common themes.

The three (or more) columns serve as a meaningful space, a set of "empty buckets" that people can use to sort their ideas, kind of like a cubbyhole desk or one of those change-sorting machines you see sometimes at carnivals.

AFFINITY MAPPING.

Having a business meeting without artifacts and meaningful space is like meeting blindfolded with your hands behind your back. Yes, you can do it, but why would you want to?

6. Sketching and Model Making

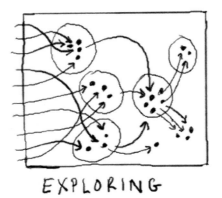

EXPLORING

Sketches and models are kinds of artifacts. A sketch can be a drawing, as in a pencil sketch. It can be a short skit, as in a comedy sketch. It can be a roughly described outline, as in "he sketched out a plan" or "she sketched in the details." What do all these meanings have in common? What is the nature of a sketch?

The defining characteristics of a sketch are its informality, looseness, and brevity. A sketch is a preliminary activity that may or may not lead to a more refined, finished version. A sketch is a rapid study, an exploration. An artist might do hundreds of sketches before settling on one idea for deeper examination. Sketching is a way to quickly explore ideas by making them more tangible or concrete.

A good sketch has just enough information to get an idea across, and no more. But sketching out ideas cannot be the sole domain of the artist, sculptor, or actor. Most of us convey our thoughts verbally or in writing, but this is only one channel of communication, and limiting our ideas to a single channel is a serious constraint on thinking.

Pythagoras, Euclid, Descartes, and Newton would never have made their discoveries without the use of pictures and diagrams. Einstein said his thinking relied on images of "a visual and muscular type."

A quick introduction to visual language (for example, see the Visual Alphabet discussion in Chapter 3) should help most people over the barrier so that they can feel comfortable expressing ideas visually or symbolically. Sketching can also include other kinds of modeling exercises, such as a quick improvised skit or physical model making with Plasticine clay and pipe cleaners. The key is to make things real with minimal effort. Rapid paper prototyping is a way to sketch software interfaces. Designers create mockups of computer interfaces using sticky notes, paper, and cardboard, which they can then use to test and try out various user interactions.

7. Randomness, Reversal, and Reframing

Not everything comes to us in order. It's rumored that William S. Burroughs determined the order of the pages in his book, *Naked Lunch*, by throwing the manuscript in the air and assembling the pages in the order he picked them up. The Qur'an was revealed to Mohammed in sections, and only later did he determine their proper order. The human brain is a pattern-making machine. We seek and find patterns everywhere we look. Leonardo da Vinci used to find inspiration by looking at stains on the wall:

> *I cannot forbear to mention...a new device for study...which may seem trivial and almost ludicrous...[but] is extremely useful in arousing the mind...Look at a wall spotted with stains, or with a mixture of stones... you may discover a resemblance to landscapes...battles with figures in action...strange faces and costumes...and an endless variety of objects....* —Leonardo da Vinci

We are so good at finding patterns that once we find one, it can be difficult to see anything else. Creating randomness is a way of fooling the mind so that you can more easily search for new patterns in familiar domains. By shuffling the deck, reversing the order, or reframing the familiar, you create enough space for new ideas and opportunities to emerge.

Randomness is an essential element in any kind of creativity. The shuffling and recombination of genes, for example, is an essential element in the variation and selection that leads to the emergence of new life forms. The same principle works in the realm of thought and ideas.

A map of the world with south at the top, for example, invites new thinking about the relationships between nations.

One reason to use modular artifacts such as index cards and sticky notes is that they facilitate randomness; they can be easily shuffled, re-sorted, and rearranged to generate new patterns and ideas.

8. Improvisation

To improvise is to make it up as you go along, to make do with whatever happens to be available, to proceed without a plan. Like a jazz musician, you compose and create simultaneously. When you improvise, you create in the moment, responding intuitively to the environment and your inner feelings. You let go. By letting go of your assumptions and biases, you open a path to new ideas, new practices, and new behaviors. You consciously forget what you know in order to elicit spontaneity, serendipity, and surprise.

Improvisation is a way of thinking with your body. In role play, you take on the role of a character, imagine a situation, and act as you think your character would act in that situation. Putting yourself in another person's shoes helps you to empathize with that person's goals and challenges, and can lead to insights and better solutions.

Bodystorming (see game description in Chapter 4) is a kind of improvisation in which players construct (sketch) a makeshift world using cardboard, chairs, or whatever is at hand, and then act out scenarios within that world in order to understand it better.

In the early 1990s, user experience designer Jared Spool and several colleagues developed a design game in which players worked together to design a prototype of an interactive kiosk using cardboard and paper. The purpose of the game was to help designers learn how paper prototyping could speed up their design process.

Because of the fleeting, impermanent nature of the ideas generated by these kinds of exercises, it can be very helpful to have some recording equipment handy, such as a video camera, a small tripod, and perhaps a microphone. If you plan to be doing a lot of this you may want to invest in more professional equipment. There's a balance to be struck here: while recording sessions is a way to create tangible artifacts that represent temporal experiences, it may also take some of the spontaneity out of the improvisation. You can read more about improvisation in Chapter 3.

9. Selection

You can't do everything, and so there are times when you will need to winnow a large set of ideas or options down to a smaller, more manageable set.

Voting can be a good way to do this. We're all familiar with raising our hands or using a secret ballot to vote on things, but when you have a massive amount of information that you need to cull, there are better, faster ways to use voting to do this. For example, you can give everyone 10 small, round stickers and ask them to stick them on the things that interest them most. When they are out of stickers they are out of votes.

Voting with stickers (as in the Dot Voting game in Chapter 4) is an example of a form of currency. Circular stickers are like money that players can distribute among a group of things, to help them decide what matters most to them. Imagine your grocery list again, and imagine that you have a very long list but a limited amount of money. If you had unlimited funds, you could buy everything you wanted, but the fact that your funds are limited forces you to make choices—sometimes difficult ones.

People have a natural tendency to bite off more than they can chew. We are naturally optimistic. But when people do this they easily become overwhelmed and then nothing is accomplished in the end. Voting and currencies help people make the difficult choices about what is important to them. By giving people stickers, or asking them to make marks that represent their votes, you can make the preferences of a group visible and explicit so that they can see where everybody stands and move more quickly to decisions.

Another way to boil down a set of ideas is to sort information according to priority. Forced Ranking (see Chapter 4) prioritizes a list of items by "forcing" them into a linear rank: most important to least important, first to last, and so on. For example, imagine your grocery list again. You could force-rank the list by organizing items by cost, from most expensive to least expensive. You could also force-rank the items in order of priority, from most important to least important. If you have a limited amount of money to spend you could compare both lists to determine the best way to spend your money.

10. Try Something New

The best way to hone your knowledge in exploring skills is to keep yourself honest. You won't discover and invent anything unless you get used to taking risks and trying new things on a regular basis. Make it a practice to try at least one new thing every time you gamestorm. It will keep you honest, force you to continuously develop and improve, and keep things fresh and alive for you. You won't inspire others unless you can stoke your own fires.

Think of gamestorming as a toolkit that allows you to plug pieces together in different ways, depending on the way the action is going. The game is the game until it changes. A seasoned knowledge explorer will quickly abandon a game that isn't working and smoothly transition into another. You can think of each game as a scene in a play—or a skit. The players need to have their heads in the game to make real, meaningful progress.

In a gamestorming environment you might move from a role-playing game to a board game to a building game in quick succession. The games are not ends in themselves, but building blocks that help you get from one point to another. Like a team of soldiers building a pontoon bridge to cross a river, you create a game when you need it, use it for as long as it is useful, and then discard it when you no longer need it. It's like building a ladder one step at a time because you aren't quite sure where you're going; like a cartoon character building a ladder to nowhere.

Be in the now. Look around and grab something, patch it together, make a game from the simplest tools. The game will move you forward. You don't need to know the final destination; only the next step in the journey. Just keep your eye on the fuzzy goal—the mountaintop, the imagined thing over the horizon—and the next step, the next game, that moves you one step in approximately the right direction.

CHAPTER 3

Core Gamestorming Skills

AT THIS POINT, IF YOU FEEL READY, YOU MIGHT WANT TO FLIP to the games section of the book and read a few of the games, or maybe try a few with some friends or colleagues. If not, and you'd like to learn more about gamestorming skills, keep reading. In this chapter, we will take a closer look at some of the essentials and how they work, namely:

Questions: The core fire-starting skill that ignites the initial spark

Artifacts and meaningful space: The boards and playing pieces that form the backbone of most games

Visual language: The ability to make your imagination and ideas more tangible and sharable

Improvisation: The ability to explore experiences with your whole self; your heart and body as well as your mind

If you're ready, let's dive in.

Asking Questions

Perhaps nothing is more important to exploration and discovery than the art of asking good questions. Questions are fire-starters: they ignite people's passions and energy; they create heat; and they illuminate things that were previously obscure.

In life and in business, we are often in a position where we want to go from point A to point B. When the path from A to B is clear, we can draw a straight line and be done with it. Whether that path is easy or difficult is beside the point.

A   B

A question is one half of an equation, where the other half is usually unknown. If the question is "How do we get from here to there?" and the answer is known, the equation is fulfilled and we have our answer. We can draw a straight line from A to B. This is the process answer, where we describe the path from A to B as a series of steps.

When the path from A to B is unclear, we have a different kind of challenge. If we ask the same question, "How do we get from here to there?" we need to face the fact that we don't know the answer. The answer in fact may be not only unknown but also unknowable: not all questions are answerable.

Crossing this kind of challenge space is a journey into the unknown, like crossing a desert or sailing into uncharted waters. When you begin, it's impossible to know how near or far the answer—if there is an answer—may be. There are five kinds of questions for finding your way in complex challenge spaces: opening, navigating, examining, experimental, and closing questions.

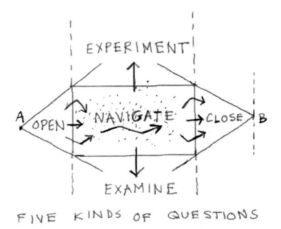

FIVE KINDS OF QUESTIONS

As we've seen, in any knowledge game you must open the world, explore the world, and close the world. In between points A and B you must navigate as best you can to ensure that you are making the progress you want.

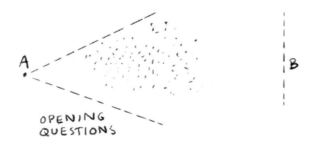

OPENING
QUESTIONS

Opening Questions

Opening questions are intended to open a portal into the game world. The opening stage of your game is the first act, where the players get to know each other and, together, you identify the main themes you want to explore in the next stage. The trick of opening is to get people to feel comfortable with the process of working together while generating as many ideas as possible. If they know each other too well, they will have trouble breaking out of the traditional limits of their collective culture and their ideas will be too similar. If they are complete strangers, they will generate a lot of diverse ideas but may have trouble working together as a team.

The idea behind an opening question is to generate ideas and options, to provoke thought and reveal possibilities, to jump-start the brain. Good opening questions open doors to new ways of looking at a challenge. The feeling you are striving for is a sense of energy and optimism, where anything is possible. A good opening is a call to adventure.

For example, you might start by brainstorming a list of questions about the challenge space. Focus on quantity, not quality. Withhold criticism and welcome unusual or controversial ideas. Look to build on ideas and combine them to make them better.

The focus of opening questions is to find things you can work with later. Imagine yourself with a big basket that can hold an infinite number of ideas. If you find something, don't ask if it's useful; just put it into the basket. The more ideas and variation you have, the better.

Here are some examples of opening questions:

- "How would you define the problem we are facing?"
- "What kinds of things do we want to explore?"
- "What are the biggest problem areas?"

Navigating Questions

Navigating questions help you assess and adjust your course while the game is underway. For example, summarize key points and confirm that people agree to ensure that you understand and that the group is aligned.

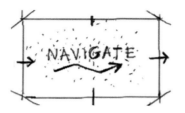

Is the team fatigued? Are they frustrated or sapped of energy? Take a break and check in. Ask them questions that will help them see how difficult the problem is or how far they have come.

Are you getting where you need to go? Have you made as much progress as you had hoped? Are people still feeling connected to the project? Ask them!

Before you ask too many navigating questions, keep in mind that you may have more experience navigating complex challenge spaces than some of the other people in the room. You may have a better sense of how far along you are than they do. If you are the captain of the ship, it may make people nervous if you express too much doubt.

Navigating questions set the course, point the way, and adjust for error. Here are some examples of navigating questions:

- "Are we on track?"

- "Did I understand this correctly?"

- "Is this helping us to get where we want to go?"

- "Is this a useful discussion thread?"

- "Should we table this for now and put it on a list of things to talk about later?"

- "Does the goal that we set this morning still make sense, or should we make some adjustments based on what we have learned so far?"

There are two big questions that are worth asking whenever you come across something new. First, what is it? And second, what can I do with it? The first question has to do with examination, while the second deals with experimentation.

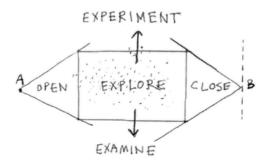

Examining Questions

Examining questions invoke observation and analysis. What is it? What is its nature? The more closely you look at something the better you can examine it. Examining questions narrow your inquiry to focus on details, specifics, and observable characteristics. They make abstract ideas more concrete by quantifying and qualifying them. You can imagine an examining question as a lens that allows you to zoom in to a topic so that you can see more detail. Usually it's good to begin an exploration by examining and challenging your fundamental assumptions.

> *If your idea were a rock, examining questions would help you under-*
> *stand things like its weight, color, size, shape, and chemical makeup.*

Here are some examples of examining questions:

- "What is it made of?"

- "How does it work?"

- "What are the pieces and parts?"

- "Can you give me an example of that?"

- "What does that look like?"

- "Can you describe it in terms of a real-life scenario?"

Experimental Questions

Experimental questions invoke the imagination. They are about possibility. What can we do with it? What opportunities does it create? Experimental questions are concerned with taking you to a higher level of abstraction to find similarities with other things, to make unlikely and unexpected connections. Whatever "it" is, experiment with it. Try to break it, throw it, spin it, invert it, and so on.

If your idea were a rock, experimental questions would ask "What can I do with this that's beyond the obvious?" For example, you could use it to hammer a nail, or you could throw it, make noise with it, and so on. One day someone asked questions like this, came up with the idea for the pet rock, and made a million dollars.

Here are some examples of experimental questions:

- "What else works like this?"

- "If this were an animal (or a plant, machine, etc.), what kind of animal would it be, and why?"

- "What are we missing?"

- "What if all the barriers were removed?"

- "How would we handle this if we were operating a restaurant? What if it was a hospital?"

- "What if we are wrong?"

You can think of this as a matter of altitude. When people are getting too caught up in the details, spark the imagination and bring them up a level with some experimental questions. If they are up in the clouds and need a bit of grounding, bring them down with some examining questions.

Closing Questions

Closing questions serve the opposite function from opening questions. When you are opening you want to create as much divergence and variation as possible. When you are closing you want to focus on convergence and selection. Your goal at this stage is to move toward commitment, decisions, and action. Opening is about opportunities; closing is about selecting which opportunities you want to pursue. That means eliminating lines of inquiry that don't seem promising, assigning priorities, and so on. Now is the time for critical thinking.

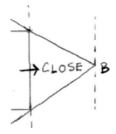

Closing is like coming home. You are tired but you want to end the day with a sense of accomplishment. What have you achieved? What have you accomplished? The natural need for a feeling of accomplishment is one of the reasons why tangible outcomes are so important in gamestorming. The fact that people have created something tangible—even if it's simply a report or to-do list—helps the group maintain momentum and generate energy for the next phase of activity.

People want to know: Where is the artifact? What is finished? What comes next? What will tomorrow look like?

Here are some examples of closing questions:

- "How can we prioritize these options?"
- "What's feasible?"
- "What can we do in the next two weeks?"
- "Who is going to do what?"

Creating Artifacts and Meaningful Space

In 1968, Dr. Spencer Silver, a scientist at 3M, developed a low-tack, reusable adhesive. For years, he promoted it within the company in the hope of turning it into a product. The adhesive was strong enough to hold papers together but weak enough that they could easily be pulled apart without tearing. He promoted it as a spray, or as a surface for bulletin boards where papers could be attached and removed without the use of pins.

Silver was not having much luck promoting his invention until he ran into Arthur Fry, who sang in his church choir and was frustrated that the small slips of paper he used as bookmarks kept falling out of his hymnal. Fry realized that the adhesive was perfect for keeping his bookmarks attached to the hymnal without damaging the book. And thus the Post-it and many sticky-note progeny were born.

The sticky note is one of the most useful tools for knowledge work because it allows you to break any complex topic into small, movable artifacts—knowledge atoms or nodes—that you can then distribute into physical space by attaching them to your desk, walls, doors, and so on without wreaking total havoc. This allows you to quickly and easily explore all kinds of relationships between and among the atoms, and to keep these various alternatives within your visual field while you are working.

It's easy to see the value of being able to distribute information into your environment in this way by looking at all the ways people use sticky notes in their daily lives. Want to remember to bring something to work? Leave a sticky note on the inside of the front door to remind you. Want to remember which items to pick up on the way home? Leave a sticky note on your phone. Need to remember how to get somewhere? Write the directions on a sticky note and stick it to your steering wheel. Want to leave a message for someone at work? Leave a sticky note on her computer screen.

Placing artifacts into the environment like this is a way to put ideas into context in a way that's dynamic. Combinations can stay fixed for as long as you want them to, and can also be shuffled or reconfigured at a moment's notice.

Artifacts like sticky notes and index cards have the same kinds of properties as a deck of cards. They can be spread out in various combinations. They can be shuffled into random order. They can be distributed into groups. Endless permutations and combinations are possible.

Nodes

We can call any artifact we generate a *node*, that is, anything considered part of a larger system.

So, you have generated a bunch of nodes—most likely index cards and sticky notes or some combination of them—and you want to explore some different combinations. What do you do? You can shuffle them. You can group them by sorting them into piles or clusters (a cluster is simply a pile that's spread out so that you can see everything in the pile).

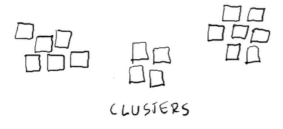

CLUSTERS

PILES

Linking

Another way to organize nodes is to link them together in various ways, in much the same way as the World Wide Web is organized by the links that connect pages and ideas to one another. For example, you could link nodes together in a chain that represents a process, like a flowchart, or link them conceptually, such as you might do in a mind map. With sticky notes and a whiteboard, you can start to create flows and structures like these:

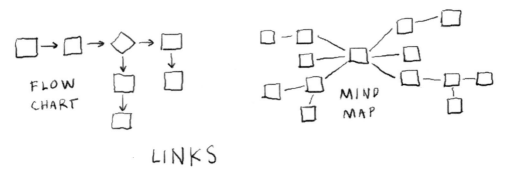

Now let's add to this equation the concept of meaningful, organized space, such as what you might find in a board game, or on a tennis court, or golf course. Think about what these organized spaces make possible: they allow the position of artifacts to have a precise meaning that is dependent on their position.

Borders

Borders are lines that frame a space. They create edges that separate one thing from another. A border can be as simple as a line down the center of the page that separates the pros from the cons. By drawing a box or a circle you create a border that separates the inside from the outside. Borders are imaginary lines. You can see borders on a map, but if you go to the real place that's represented on the map, you won't see a line drawn on the ground. Nevertheless, borders are so important that for many people they are worth fighting wars over.

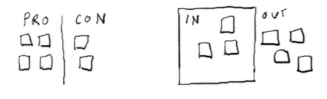

Axes

An axis gives meaning to direction within a space. One common example is the compass points on a map. By convention, north is usually up unless otherwise noted. Now, in addition to the borders that separate the countries, we have a common language for navigating within the space.

Unlike a border, which simply separates one thing from another, an axis is a line of force. It has direction. North may be indicated by a small arrow in the corner of a map, but nevertheless the idea influences the entire map. North is "up" not only in the corner, but all over the map.

Like the north arrow on a map, many axes are not explicitly depicted but are implied by convention. For example, in Western countries people read left to right, so when you do something like place a bunch of sticky notes in a left-to-right sequence, many people will assume that you intend them to be read in sequence. Similarly, if you organize things from top to bottom, many people will assume that you have ranked them in order of importance (at least, in the West).

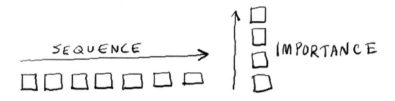

Many methods for organizing ideas have implied axes that are not explicitly depicted. The org chart, for example, has an implied axis where up represents "reports to" and down represents "authority over"; and the conference brackets in a sports tournament have an implied time axis that goes from left to right.

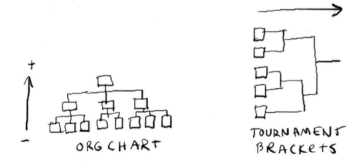

Circles and Targets

Circles and target shapes can be useful when you want to approximate how close you are to a stated goal. Like an archer shooting arrows at a target, you can estimate how close or how far a certain artifact is from the center you are aiming for. You can use concentric rings and axes in combination to delineate both degree and lines of force.

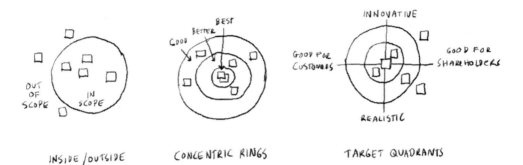

Metric Versus Ordered Space

To illustrate the difference between metric and ordered space, think about how we measure time. When we talk about the days of the week or the months of the year, we are making an either/or kind of distinction. "What day is it?" is an either/or question. Either it's Monday, or it's Tuesday, and so on. When we talk about the time of day we are talking about something that's much more relative and is dependent on who is asking the question and in what context. We might answer "noonish" or we might answer "12:01:36," depending on the context. That's because calendar time is ordered (we care more about sequence than precision) and clock time is measured (we care more about precision than sequence).

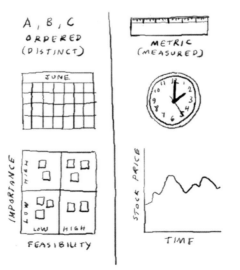

Metric space is space that we measure with more or less precision. Ordered space is space where we care more about the order of things than their precise position. For example, in a footrace it's usually very important who came in first, second, and third. The exact times may be important also, but probably less so. If the first-place runner came in an hour before the second-place runner, and the second-place runner came in only minutes before the third-place runner, the order of their finishing is the same as though they all finished within seconds of each other. In meaningful space that's metric, we care about things that are absolute, like height, weight, length, distance, speed, temperature, and so on. In meaningful space that's ordered, we care more about categories and relationships: Is it higher or lower? Heavier or lighter? Longer or shorter? And so on.

Grids

The grid is simply what you see when you look at a chessboard, checkerboard, spreadsheet, or soldiers on parade. Rows and columns, rank and file. The file or column is the vertical line. When people march in single file, it means they have lined up in a column, like the lines you see in the grocery store or the bank. The row or rank is the horizontal line. In combination, rank and file make up a grid, one of the most useful methods for organizing information.

Grids come in all shapes and sizes. You can use grids to organize physical space, such as the gridlines on a map. You can use a grid to formulate a search, such as in the game of Battleship. You can use a grid to lay out a web page or a magazine page. You can use it to do your bookkeeping, or to organize any set of numbers into columns and rows. One very useful form of grid is to break a square into quadrants to organize information according to two criteria. Another useful method is to use a grid to sort things into columns or rows.

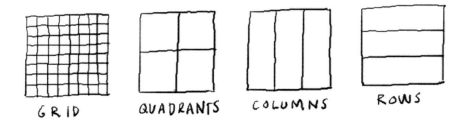

GRID   QUADRANTS   COLUMNS   ROWS

Landscapes and Maps

Sometimes it makes sense to think of information in terms of a landscape. Every business is on a journey of some kind, going from one place to another, and every marketplace is a landscape with its own unique perils, challenges, and opportunities. What journey is your business on? What does the road ahead look like? What obstacles lie in the immediate future? What is farther down the road? What forces help drive you forward? What forces hold you back?

David Sibbet, of The Grove Consultants International, uses a tool he calls the Graphic Gameplan to help teams think through their challenges. The Graphic Gameplan uses a precisely designed set of meaningful spaces to organize people's thinking and move from ideas to action. Challenges are represented as a rough landscape, actions as an arrow, success factors as wheels, goals as a target, and so on.

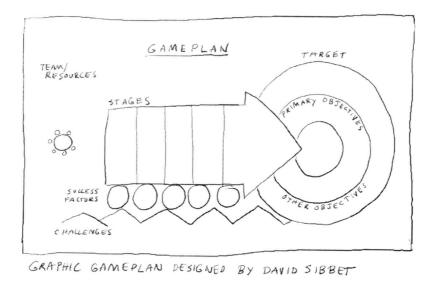

GRAPHIC GAMEPLAN DESIGNED BY DAVID SIBBET

The Graphic Gameplan is one of many Graphic Guide® templates designed by David Sibbet of The Grove Consultants International. You can order templates at http://www.grove.com/site/index.html.

Metaphor

Another way to organize information is to formulate analogies and conceptual links with other things. Your information space can be represented by a house, an airplane, a building, an animal, a ship, a restaurant, or anything else that will help you break out of habitual thinking patterns. A good metaphor comes with a set of associations that will change your perspective and help you think differently about a topic. A metaphoric structure can help you ask new and thought-provoking questions that you may not have considered before.

For example, a house is a common metaphor that leads to questions such as: What are the foundations? What are the columns and beams that support the roof? What covers us? What is the floor, the walls?

WHERE WE CAME FROM

WHAT GIVES US THE POWER?

WHERE WE ARE GOING

WHO DO WE DELIVER VALUE TO?

HOW DO WE STEER?

One danger in this kind of exploration is getting too connected to, or too rigid about, the metaphor—everything does not need to force-fit into the metaphor.

For example, I once worked with a recruiting company and we were using fishing as a metaphor for recruiting. That's a solid metaphor and it's useful as long as it generates thought-provoking questions. But you're sinking too low when you start asking questions like: Does this mean we see the people we are recruiting as food? That we are baiting them and that they will end up worse off? No, it doesn't. It's a metaphor, a tool for thinking. Don't let people overthink it or you'll go down a rabbit hole.

Employing Visual Language

In school we are taught that the fundamental things we need to learn to be successful in our society are reading, writing, and arithmetic. The first several years of public education focus primarily on these fundamentals. In an industrial world, where every worker functioned as a standardized cog in a corporate machine, this may have made sense.

But today's challenges aren't standard. As we have discussed, work today often must address unknowns, uncertainty, and ambiguous challenge spaces where solutions are not clear or standard, and where the ability to create and discover is more important than fitting a standard mold.

Our world has a rich history of creation and discovery. We have discovered the shape of the world, the elements of matter, and the laws that govern the movements of the stars. We have created technologies that can make us fly, allow us to talk to each other and see each other from anywhere in the world, and can move information at the speed of light. So, it's not hard for us to look at the people who have discovered and created these miracles and ask, "What methods did they use?"

Yes, reading, writing, and arithmetic were instrumental in many of these monumental achievements. The written word and mathematics are both powerful tools. They are languages that we can use to make conceptual models, think about the world, and convey complex ideas to each other. But there is another language that's equally powerful, and we don't teach it in schools—at least, not consistently and not very well. It's called visual language, and it's the language we use to make ideas visual and explicit.

The great voyages of Columbus, Magellan, and James Cook would not have been possible without advanced map-making capabilities. The mathematical advances of Euclid, Descartes, and Newton would not have been conceivable without the use of pictorial diagrams. The inventions of Leonardo da Vinci, Thomas Edison, and Tim Berners-Lee— the man who invented the Internet—were possible only because these people had the ability to visualize and draw their ideas. Nearly every human endeavor, when examined, reveals evidence of the importance of visual language. In legal proceedings, visual aids help juries decide complex cases. Filmmakers create storyboards to help them bring screenplays to life. Medical illustration helps surgeons and other medical professionals learn their trade. The road signs we navigate by, the interfaces on our computer screens, and the logos that help us find the stores and brands we like are all examples of visual language in action. Even your driver's license would be useless without the image that represents you and confirms that, yes, the person in the picture is in fact the person this card identifies.

We've listed sketching as one of the 10 essentials of gamestorming—it's an important element of creative thinking, and anyone can do it. You don't need any special skills. You can start with a pen and paper. That doesn't mean it's easy, any more than reading, writing, and arithmetic are easy; you will need to apply yourself. But we have found that the biggest hurdle for most people is confidence. If you can bring yourself to dive in and start drawing, the rest will take care of itself. So, with that in mind, here are a few concepts and exercises that you can use to start building some basic drawing skills. Once you are familiar with these concepts you can use the same exercises to bring colleagues and other groups quickly up to speed.

Now, grab a pen and a piece of paper and let's do a few exercises.

The Visual Alphabet

Let's begin with the visual alphabet, a kind of proto-alphabet of visual shapes that you can use to construct any kind of visual. It's made up of 12 shapes—the "letters" of the visual alphabet—called glyphs. If you can draw these 12 shapes you can draw anything else you can imagine.

The first six glyphs are linear. They can be linked to each other in a sequence or chain; they are open shapes that flow naturally together, so we call them flows. Their names are point, line, angle, arc, spiral, and loop. Try drawing them now.

The next six glyphs are closed shapes. When a line closes in on itself it tends to feel more like a solid object, because the border of a closed shape separates it from the background, like an island. Closed shapes are distinct from the environment that surrounds them, which gives them the illusion of form, so we call these shapes forms. Their names are oval, eye, triangle, rectangle, house, and cloud. Try drawing them now.

$$\bigcirc \; \diamondsuit \; \triangle \; \square \; \bigtriangleup \; \diamondsuit$$

With these 12 glyphs you can draw anything. The number of possible combinations is infinite. Hard to believe? Let's prove this in a few steps. First, see if you can make the letters of the alphabet using just the 12 shapes of the visual alphabet:

A B C D E F G H I J K L M N O P Q R S T U V W X Y Z

Satisfied? From 12 come 26. And now the numbers:

1 2 3 4 5 6 7 8 9 0

Now let's try something more difficult. Look around you, wherever you happen to be at the moment. Pick out a few simple objects and see if you can draw them using just the shapes from the visual alphabet:

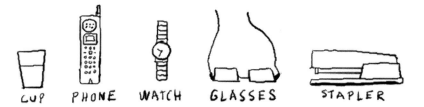

CUP   PHONE   WATCH   GLASSES   STAPLER

Notice that the images in the preceding figure are labeled. Pictures don't need to carry all the semantic weight of whatever you are trying to convey. This is a key difference between drawing and visual language. Drawing in an artistic sense is about fooling the eye—making things appear like they appear in nature. Visual language is about conveying meaning. By labeling anything that might be otherwise ambiguous or confusing, you make it easier for people to understand what you are "drawing about."

Drawing People

Now let's try something a little more difficult. One of the most common things you'll need to draw, since you'll be communicating with people, is, yes, people. Just about anything you want to communicate visually will probably require images of people at one point or another.

Most of us can use the glyphs of the visual alphabet to draw a simple stick figure, like this:

The problem arises when you try to draw something more complex, such as people doing something more than just standing there. Usually when you want to draw a person, it's because you want to show an action—for example, somebody eating dinner, using a vending machine, driving a car, or riding a bicycle.

Let's start by drawing a picture of somebody mailing a letter.

First, imagine yourself mailing a letter. Pick up a piece of paper and pose yourself in that position to see how it feels. You might want to do it in front of a mirror or ask a friend to take a picture at first. Or if it's easier, you can find a picture on the Internet or in a magazine. Over time, with practice you will be able to imagine and draw people without posing or reference.

Pay special attention to the angle of the body; it conveys the essence of the action. Think about what you notice first when you see a person in the distance. It's the position of the body that conveys a person's attitude as much as anything else. Most people draw a stick figure by starting with the head and adding the body afterward. This way of drawing a stick figure will almost always result in a big-headed, stiff stick figure.

When drawing a person, you will get a much better effect if you start with the center of gravity and work outward. Draw a rectangle to represent the trunk of the body, trying to keep it at approximately the same angle.

In his notebooks, Leonardo da Vinci kept careful notes about the importance of the body's attitude and how it can be used to convey meaning:

> A picture or representation of human figures ought to be done in such a way as that the spectator may easily recognize, by means of their attitudes, the purpose in their minds. Thus, if you have to represent a man of noble character in the act of speaking, let his gestures be such as naturally accompany good words; and, in the same way, if you wish to depict a man of a brutal nature, give him fierce movements; as with his arms flung out towards the listener, and his head and breast thrust forward beyond his feet, as if following the speaker's hands. Thus it is with a deaf and dumb person who, when he sees two men in conversation—although he is deprived of hearing—can nevertheless understand, from the attitudes and gestures of the speakers, the nature of their discussion."—Leonardo da Vinci

The next most prominent feature is the legs; they connect the person to the ground and have the most impact on the body's position. Draw a line to represent the ground and add lines for the legs and feet to connect the body to the ground.

The next most important element to conveying attitude is the hands. We use our hands for nearly everything we do. Have you ever heard the advice given to public speakers to use their hands and to gesture to help them reinforce their meaning? The same principle applies to stick figures. Now try drawing the arms in position. A small circle is usually sufficient to represent the hands. Don't forget to add the letter, or our trip to the mailbox will be wasted.

Now take a look at the angle of the neck and head relative to the rest of the body. Notice that they are at different angles. Unless you are a soldier standing at attention, this is nearly always the case. We are constantly turning our heads to see better, to listen carefully, and so on. See if you can draw the head and attach it to the body with a single line at the right angle.

Now that we have finished the figure we can think about the face. Think about the various smiley faces and other emoticons you can make on a computer keyboard. Those same combinations will suffice for nearly any facial expression you want. Adding a short line for the nose will help you show which direction the head is pointing. This can be especially important when you want to show two people interacting with each other.

You can use the same principles you learned earlier to make the mailbox, by combining basic shapes from the visual alphabet. I live in the United States, where our mailboxes look like R2-D2 of Star Wars fame. Depending on where you live, yours may differ.

I hope this short demonstration has convinced you that basic sketching skills are not out of your reach. Once you become comfortable with the preceding exercises, you can use them to help others become more comfortable with sketching their ideas. In numerous workshops, I have found that you can get through these exercises with a group in about 10 to 15 minutes. In the time it takes for a brief coffee break you can familiarize a group with these concepts and get them comfortable enough to begin sketching out their ideas.

Perspective

One thing that often intimidates people is the notion of perspective. I have found it helpful to describe the three primary methods that have been used to create a sense of visual space in the history of art. The one we are most familiar with is linear perspective, developed during the Italian renaissance. The invention, or perhaps I should say "discovery," of perspective is credited to the artist and architect Filippo Brunnelleschi around 1425.

Linear perspective creates the illusion of space by imitating the view seen by the eye from a particular vantage point. The artist draws a line representing the horizon at eye level and then establishes vanishing points along that horizon. You can use these vanishing points to construct almost any scene and give an illusion of depth which immerses the viewer in the scene.

But linear perspective is only one of three principal methods that artists have used through the centuries.

Parallel perspective is another form of pictorial grammar that originated in China and predates linear perspective by hundreds of years. In parallel perspective, construction lines do not converge to points on the horizon, but are drawn parallel to each other so that the scene appears to go on indefinitely in all directions. This is a way of showing a scene as though seen from above, and has the advantage that everything in the image can be drawn to the same scale. This is sometimes called God's perspective because of the aerial view that can be extended infinitely in all directions.

An even earlier form of pictorial space emerged thousands of years before either linear or parallel perspective. This way of organizing images was more similar to written language and perhaps found its purest expression in the art of ancient Egypt, so I like to call this Egyptian perspective. Instead of drawing things as we see them, it involved drawing things in their ideal form, as they might be seen by the mind. If something was most recognizable from the side, it was drawn in profile; if it was most recognizable from the top, it was drawn from that perspective. This Egyptian form of perspective is by far the most common across all societies and cultures since the earliest times. Children will naturally draw things this way unless they are taught a different method. For many uses it is the clearest and easiest to understand, and for most people it's the easiest to learn and apply quickly.

To draw in the Egyptian perspective, all you need to do is think like a child. Draw things the way they appear in your mind's eye, without worrying about whether they resemble reality. The idea in Egyptian perspective is to capture and convey the essence of the object. A drawing of a cat doesn't need to look like a cat so much as it must convey the idea of a cat. The letters in the word *CAT* convey an idea without any resemblance whatsoever, and you can convey the same concept pictorially with a very small number of simple shapes.

THERE'S MORE THAN ONE WAY TO SKETCH A CAT!

How many ways can you sketch a cat?

As you begin to develop your visual language skills, consider carrying a notebook, as Leonardo da Vinci did, to record your observations and reflections. Here's his advice on the matter:

> *Go about, and constantly, as you go, observe, note and consider the circumstances and behavior of men in talking, quarreling or laughing or fighting together; the action of the men themselves and the actions of the bystanders, who separate them or look on. And take a note of them with slight strokes in a little book which you should always carry with you… for the forms, and positions of objects are so infinite that the memory is incapable of retaining them, wherefore keep these [sketches] as your guides and masters. —Leonardo da Vinci*

Improvisation

If anything most resembles gamestorming in its purest form, surely it's improvisation. As a group, the players work together to create a world and explore it with their intuition and their entire bodies.

Improvisation is a big word with lots of meanings—it means different things to different people and in different contexts.

When you are faced with the unexpected, to improvise is to be in the moment, to proceed without a plan. It is to make do with whatever is at hand, to use your ingenuity to develop makeshift solutions to unanticipated problems. Thus, improvisation skills are survival skills. It's a common problem for any explorer: when you don't know what to expect and you need to anticipate anything and everything, what do you bring?

In jazz and theater traditions, improvisation involves laying out a basic structure and then creating spontaneous compositions that weave within and around that structure to create harmonious, beautiful, and sometimes complex sounds and scenarios. In this context, improvisation's beauty lies in its spontaneity and variety.

For knowledge explorers, improvisation is important in both ways—the ability to quickly respond to unanticipated or emergency situations as well as to develop spontaneous compositions around a baseline rhythm or structure. We'll take both in turn.

> **Responsiveness to the unexpected:** The 10 essentials are a great set of methods that will apply to nearly any unexpected situation. If you have your core supplies handy (flip charts, markers, sticky notes, dot voting, paper, index cards), and you have mastered the core skills (questions, use of artifacts and meaningful space, sketching and improvisation), it will be a rare circumstance that will throw you off your feet. There's a great calm and confidence that comes from knowing that you have the tools as well as the skills, and are prepared for any situation.

> **Variations on a theme:** Like almost the entire gamestorming toolkit, improvisation is a matter of some basic skills combined with a lot of practice. It is the goal of this section to lay out some basic principles and practices that will help you create simple, loose structures and guide people through the process of exploring them improvisationally—that is, with the kind of spontaneity and freedom that involves the physical senses in the process of discovery, and develops and hones the intuitive sense.

The idea of bringing improv into a business context may seem intimidating, but the challenges are mostly in your mind. You're already improvising at work. In *GameChangers: Improvisation for Business in the Networked World*, improv expert Mike Bonifer reminds us that all of life is improvisation: from a conversation at the dinner table to the way we respond to unexpected situations, improv is natural; we do it all the time.

To get people warmed up, Bonifer suggests a game he calls Gibberish. Here's how it works. Divide a group into teams of two or three people. Give the first team a slip of paper describing a scene—a role and a goal for each player—and ask them to act it out while everyone else watches. But here's the rub: they can't use words. They can only use gibberish sounds and other things like actions, body language, and tone of voice to convey their meaning. The round is over when the audience guesses what the scene is about. Do the same with each team (with different scenes, of course) until everyone has had a go.

The point of this game is to strip away what Bonifer calls the *layers of cosmetic meaning*— the talking and data that so many business conversations revolve around—in order to reveal the deeper layers of communication that are always there but often go unnoticed, like tone of voice, body language, and action.

At its core, an improv game isn't different from any other kind of gamestorming activity: you need to open the world, explore the world, and close the world. In this sense it's the same. But in another sense it's different: improv is not so much about the outcomes as it is about the experience—an experience that, hopefully, will lead to insight.

Underlying structure is important to improv in the same way that bones are helpful to muscles or trees are helpful to vines; in order to loosen up and let yourself go, you need something to innovate around or else you will simply create chaos.

Jazz musicians improvise music around a steady beat or theme. Basketball players improvise around the boundaries of the court and the rules of the game. The beauty and success of these improvisational activities would not be possible without the underlying structure that supports and contains them.

The theme is the thing you want to explore, and the scene is the thing that gives you a structure to improvise around. There are four elements of a scene: the setting, the characters, the characters' objectives, and props.

For example, let's say you want to find a way to improve the public transportation system in your city, and you want to use improv to explore some possibilities. That's your theme: getting around using public transportation.

Before you can start to improvise, you need characters, goals, settings, and props. Let's start with goals. You could brainstorm a list of situations in which people would need public transportation: one person needs to do her grocery shopping, another needs to visit a friend, another wants to see a movie or get to work. Next, you could brainstorm a list of characters. One person is retired, another is a surgeon, and so on. Now, settings: one person is at home, another is in a park. Finally, props: one person has a mobile phone, another does not.

Now, imagine that you color-code four sets of index cards so that the goals are one color, the characters are another color, and so on. You could shuffle the cards and ask people to choose one card of each color. Once everyone has his objective, you could take turns acting out the scenes. After each scene, you could have a short discussion about its implications.

One challenge with improv is that because its nature is so experiential, the learning is in the doing. An improv experience does not naturally generate a tangible artifact as an outcome. But this is not an insurmountable problem. You can assign a person to videotape the scenarios as you act them out, or ask someone to take notes or even make some storyboard sketches to capture the essence of the things you have discovered.

Practice

We can consider practice in two ways. First, we can consider practice in the sense of a profession or skill, as in a consulting practice, a law practice, or a medical practice. This can refer to a business or a core skill, as in a practice area—for example, "I practice medicine" or "My practice is in the area of urology." Second, we can discuss practice in the sense of an ongoing commitment that involves not only study but also ongoing activity to develop, hone, and maintain the skills that are necessary within a discipline. A practicing surgeon is a person who continuously works not only with her mind but also with her hands. This is the kind of practice we mean when we talk about Zen practice, or basketball practice.

Practice in the two senses mentioned here are both important and mutually interdependent. We think of a practice as something that requires long study and ongoing activity, through which, given enough of these two things, a person may achieve mastery. Mastery of a practice is not something that can be gained simply by studying a book or attending a workshop, and gamestorming is no exception to this rule. Those hoping for a "flavor of the month" to rescue their failing business, or a quick fix, can look elsewhere. But those who approach gamestorming as a practice, worthy of careful study and ongoing skill-building work, will find here a path to rich rewards and personal fulfillment at work.

In this first section of the book, we wanted to focus on the fundamentals of gamestorming and the underlying principles that make it work. We didn't want to simply write a book of recipes for people to follow blindly without understanding them. That would defeat our purpose, which is to encourage a shift in how work is done—from a process-centric model that's about predictability and consistency to a game-centric model that recognizes the complexity and unpredictability of a digital world.

In the next part of the book, we have compiled a list of the best games we know. We hope you will peruse them, try them out in your workplace, and continue to modify and improve them. If you have ideas, comments, or questions you can join the ongoing conversation at *http://www.gogamestorm.com.*

CHAPTER 4

Core Games

ONCE YOU START PLAYING AND CREATING YOUR OWN GAMES, you will likely find a short list of activities that work well in any situation. These are the reliable techniques that never let you down. They're simple enough to show up as "moves" in other games, making them a great place to start.

The 7Ps Framework

In preparing for battle I have always found that plans are useless, but planning is indispensable. —Dwight D. Eisenhower

OBJECT OF PLAY

Every meeting deserves a plan. Note that a great plan can't guarantee a great outcome, but it will help lay down the fundamentals from which you can adapt. Sketch out these fundamentals by using the 7Ps framework.

NUMBER OF PLAYERS

Individual

DURATION OF PLAY

20 minutes to 2 hours

HOW TO PLAY

Use these items as a checklist. When preparing for a meeting, thinking through the 7Ps can improve focus and results, even if you have only a few moments to reflect on them.

Purpose: Why are you having this meeting? As the leader, you need to be able to state this clearly and succinctly. Consider the urgency of the meeting: what's going on, and what's on fire? If this is difficult to articulate, ask yourself if a meeting is really necessary.

Product: What specific artifact will we produce out of the meeting? What will it do, and how will it support the purpose? If your meetings seem to be "all talk and no follow-through," consider how a product might change things.

People: Who needs to be there, and what role will they play? One way to focus your list of attendees is to think in terms of questions and answers. What questions are we answering with this meeting? Who are the right people to answer the questions?

Process: What agenda will these people use to create the product? Of all the 7Ps, the agenda is where you have the most opportunity to collaborate in advance with the attendees. Co-design an agenda with them to ensure that they will show up and stay engaged.

Pitfalls: What are the risks in this meeting, and how will we address them? These could be as simple as ground rules, such as "no laptops," or specific topics that are designated as out of scope.

Prep: What would be useful to do in advance? This could be material to read in advance, research to conduct, or "homework" to assign to the attendees.

Practical Concerns: These are the logistics of the meeting—the where and when, and importantly, who's bringing lunch.

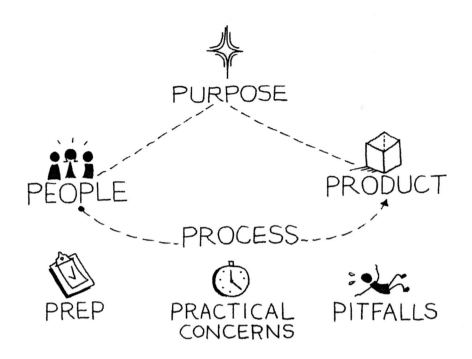

STRATEGY

- Each of the 7Ps can influence or change one of the others, and developing a good plan will take this into account. For instance, if you have certain participants for only part of a meeting, this will change your process.

- Get others involved in the design of the meeting. Their participation in its design is the quickest route to its effectiveness.

- Recurring meetings can take on a life of their own and stray from their original purpose. It's a healthy activity to revisit "Why are we having this meeting?" regularly for such events.

- Make the 7Ps visible during the meeting. These reference points can help focus and refocus a group as needed.

- Have a plan and expect it to change. The 7Ps can give you a framework for designing a meeting, but they can't run the meeting for you. The unexpected will happen, and as a leader you will need to adapt.

The 7Ps Framework is credited to James Macanufo.

Affinity Map

OBJECT OF PLAY

Most of us are familiar with brainstorming—a method by which a group generates as many ideas around a topic as possible in a limited amount of time. Brainstorming works to get a high quantity of information on the table. But it begs the follow-up question of how to gather meaning from all the data. Using a simple Affinity Diagram technique can help us discover embedded patterns (and sometimes break old patterns) of thinking by sorting and clustering language-based information into relationships. It can also give us a sense of where most people's thinking is focused. Use an affinity diagram when you want to find categories and meta-categories within a cluster of ideas and when you want to see which ideas are most common within the group.

NUMBER OF PLAYERS

Up to 20

DURATION OF PLAY

Depends on the number of players, but a maximum of 1.5 hours

HOW TO PLAY

1. On a sheet of flip-chart paper, write a question the players will respond to along with a visual that complements it. Conduct this game only when you have a question for the players that you know will generate at least 20 pieces of information to sort.

2. Ask each player to take 10 minutes to generate sticky notes in response to the question. Use index cards on a table if you have a group of four or less. Conduct this part of the process silently.

3. Collect the ideas from the group and post them on a flat working surface visible to everyone. It should end up resembling the following figure.

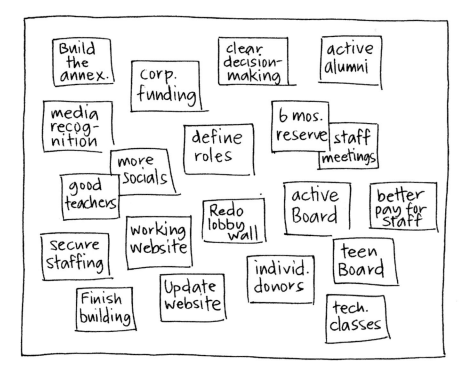

4. Based on guidance from the players, sort the ideas into columns (or clusters) based on relationships. Involve the group in the process as much as possible. Have the players approach the wall to post their notes—it saves time—and allow them to do an initial, general sorting in columns or clusters.

5. Create a sticky-note "parking lot" close to the display for ideas that don't appear to fall into a natural category. Redundancy in ideas is OK; don't discard sticky notes because they're already represented. It's helpful to leave repeated ideas posted since it indicates to the group how many people are thinking the same thing. At this stage, ask the players to try to avoid searching for higher categories and simply to focus on grouping the information based on the affinities.

6. Once the content is sorted, ask the group to suggest categories that represent the columns you've created and write the categories they agree on at the top of the column (or near a cluster if you chose a cluster rather than a column display). Don't let the players spend an inordinate amount of time agreeing on a name for a category. If there's disagreement over "Facilities" versus "Infrastructure," write them both. If the players produce categories that are significantly different, pay attention to which category gets the most approval from the group and write that one. Your visual may end up looking like the one below.

STRATEGY

The value of the Affinity Diagram game increases when two conditions are met. The first is that the players generate multiple data points, ideally with good information. The second relates to the quality of the sorting. The cleaner the players' insights when they form relationships within the content, the better the categories will be.

Fun, optional activity: Run through the Affinity Diagram game once, complete with categorizations. Then ask the group to reshuffle the sticky notes and recombine the ideas based on affinities they didn't notice in the first round.

Sometimes affinities within content are crystal clear, so the sorting becomes less pivotal, but when those relationships are more nuanced, it's more important that the sorting process is done well. In a situation in which there are many ways to affinitize information, assume a stronger facilitative role. Ask questions about the columns or clusters to clarify the group's thinking and steer them toward an appropriate number of categories. If there are too many, the data gets watered down. If there are too few, the analysis gets watered down. Help the players find the sweet spot.

The affinity diagram was devised by Jiro Kawakita in the 1960s. It is also referred to as the KJ Method.

Bodystorming

OBJECT OF PLAY

Bodystorming is simply brainstorming, but done with the body. It may look different depending on the preparations and location, but in the end all bodystorming is fundamentally about one thing: getting people to figure things out by trying things out.

A group may explore one of the techniques described below to get their feet wet with bodystorming. They may move through them in order, from observing and learning to ideation and prototyping, although this is not a strict sequence. Each level of bodystorming will help break the pattern of analyzing ideas around a conference table and get people closer to developing things that will work in the real world.

HOW TO PLAY

Bodystorming takes place in three phases.

Level 1: Go Observe

Go to the location to do your work. If you are developing an idea for a coffee shop, or a shopping mall, or a hospital, go there and do your work as you would normally. The environment will present idea cues and authentic information that would never emerge from conference room brainstorming.

For example, say a group is charged with improving the student experience on a college campus. Although they may conduct interviews or other research, they may start by going to a few campus locations and "blending in" with the surroundings while going about their usual work. It's important that the group not zero in on any specific analysis so that they will be open to the cues that the environment presents.

Level 2: Try It Out

Use role play and props to develop an idea. In this exercise, a group physically "acts out" an experience by using whatever they have on hand or can acquire. The group focuses on how they interact with each other, their surroundings, and makeshift artifacts, testing existing ideas and uncovering new ones.

For example, say a small group is asked to "reimagine the evening news." Using each other as the actors, the audience, the news anchors, and the television itself, they improvise a script that plays out the experience as they conceive it could be.

1. Identify and assign critical roles. For any experience, identifying the "customer" or "user" role is a good way to get started. This participant (or group of participants) becomes the focal point and main character of the bodystorm.

   Other critical roles will present themselves. "Who wants to be the Internet?" is not an uncommon question to hear.

2. Improvise the experience. Bodystorming is physical and progressive: as the group starts to put their thoughts into action, they will naturally ask simple and important questions by acting them out, often leading to the unexpected. For example, in the evening news scenario:

- "OK, so how do you watch the evening news?"

- "I don't have a television. Also, I'm usually out jogging."

- "Oh. Do you have your phone on you?"

- "Always. I'm listening to music."

- "OK, what if this happened… who wants to play the phone?"

- In a completely improvised scenario, the group should keep in mind the principal rule of the game: building on each other's inputs. "Yes, and…" will generate more progress than "Yeah, but…" thinking.

In some uses of bodystorming, a group will act out a script prepared in advance. In these cases, an equal amount of planning in props to build an environment is key. For example, if it's a coffee shop, set up the counter and chairs. If it's a park or outdoor area, strongly consider going there.

Level 3: Reflect on What Happens, and Why

By enacting the experience, the participants will naturally explore new possibilities, and uncover flaws or assumptions about how an idea could work. This is valuable both in the process itself and afterward: by documenting the exercise on video, the participants may later "watch the reel" to discuss key points.

STRATEGY

Choose the right level of bodystorming at the right time for the group. Because bodystorming asks participants to take a big step away from the typical conference table mode of thinking, they may need to get comfortable with more structured sessions first, armed with scripts and specific roles, before stepping into complete improv. In all cases, the exercise itself will be more memorable than the customary problem-solving session, and will help generate empathy that comes from "embodying" the experience.

The term "bodystorming" was coined by Colin Burns at CHI '94 In Boston, Massachusetts.

Card Sort

OBJECT OF PLAY

Card sorting is a practice used frequently by information architects and designers to gather and structure inputs for a variety of purposes. In a common use of card sorting, information for a website is put onto the cards, and the sorting helps create categories for navigation and the overall architecture. The method works just as well for creating slides for presentations, or at any point where information needs to be sorted and organized in a sensible way.

The applications of card sorting are numerous, and in use it works similarly to Post-Up and affinity mapping. Card sorting can differ from these methods, however. First, the cards are generally prepared in advance, although participants should be allowed to create their own while sorting. Second, the cards are a semi-permanent artifact and can be used as a control over several exercises with different participants to find patterns among them.

NUMBER OF PLAYERS

Small groups or individuals

DURATION OF PLAY

30 minutes or more, depending on the number of cards and participants

HOW TO PLAY

Use 3×5 index cards or similar. For a typical sorting exercise, aim for 30–100 cards in total; more than this range will likely overwhelm the participants, and fewer may not be meaningful enough to be worth the effort.

On each card should be a succinct bit of information; enough to tell the participants what it is and no more. Putting too much information on a card will slow down the sorting; not enough will cause confusion and will slow down the process even more.

Give the group the shuffled deck and a stack of blank cards. Describe the overall organization challenge, and ask them to sort the cards into groups that go together. If they think something is unclear or missing, they may alter a card or create a new one. Once they have created the groups, ask them to name them and describe them.

There are variations of sorting—including asking the group to rank the items from most to least desirable or to organize the cards into two categories such as "must have" and "nice to have." You may also ask the group to sort cards into a predefined set of categories, to test their validity.

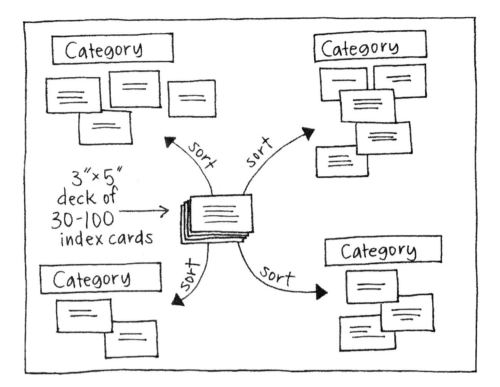

STRATEGY

Although the Card Sort game won't tell you everything you need to know about a set of information, it will help reveal the thought process of participants. In this sense, it's more about people than information. Only after a number of sorting exercises with a number of groups will larger patterns appear.

Card sorting is a common practice of information architects and designers of complex systems. Its actual source is unknown.

Dot Voting

OBJECT OF PLAY

In any good brainstorming session, there will come a time when there are too many good ideas, too many concepts, and too many possibilities to proceed. When this time has come, dot voting is one of the simplest ways to prioritize and converge upon an agreed solution.

NUMBER OF PLAYERS

At least 3 participants; in larger groups, tallying votes will be more time-consuming

DURATION OF PLAY

Short

HOW TO PLAY

First, the group needs a set of things to vote on! This may be something they have just developed, such as a wall of sticky notes, or it may be a flip-chart list that captures the ideas in one place. Ask the group to cast their votes by placing a dot next to the items they feel the most strongly about. They may use stickers or markers to do this. As a rule of thumb, giving each participant five votes to cast works well.

Participants cast their votes all at once and they may vote more than once for a single item if they feel strongly about it. Once all the votes are cast, tally them, and if necessary make a list of the items by their new rank.

This prioritized list becomes the subject of discussion and decision making. In some cases, it may be useful to reflect on ideas that didn't receive votes to verify that they haven't been left behind without cause.

STRATEGY

This technique is used to collaboratively prioritize any set of items. It could be used to hone a list of features, to agree on discussion topics, or to choose among strategies and concepts. Giving participants five votes is enough to be meaningful while still asking for individual prioritization; however, this is not a hard rule.

The original source of the Dot Voting game is unknown.

Empathy Map

OBJECT OF PLAY

The object of this game is to quickly develop a customer or user profile.

NUMBER OF PLAYERS

3–10

DURATION OF PLAY

10–15 minutes

HOW TO PLAY

Personas help focus a group's attention on the people involved in a project—often the customer or end user. Although creating an empathy map is not the rigorous, research-based process that is required for developing personas, it can quickly get a group to focus on the most important element: people.

In this exercise, you will be creating a study of a person with the group. Start by drawing a large circle that will accommodate writing inside. Add eyes and ears to make it into a large "head."

1. Ask the group to give this person a name.

2. Label large areas around the head: "Thinking", "Seeing", "Hearing", and "Feeling".

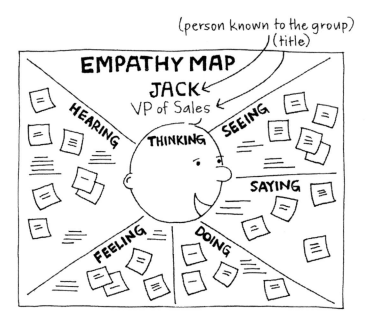

3. Ask the group to describe—from this person's point of view—what this person's experience is, moving through the categories from seeing through feeling.

4. The goal of the exercise is to create a degree of empathy for the person with the group. The exercise shouldn't take more than 15 minutes. Ask the group to synthesize: What does this person want? What forces are motivating this person? What can we do for this person?

STRATEGY

The group should feel comfortable "checking" each other by referring back to the empathy map. When this happens, it will sound like "What would so-and-so think?" It's good to keep the empathy map up and visible during the course of the work to be used as this kind of focusing device.

The Empathy Map game was developed by Scott Matthews of XPLANE.

Forced Ranking

OBJECT OF PLAY

When prioritizing, a group may need to agree on a single, ranked list of items. Forced ranking obligates the group to make difficult decisions, and each item is ranked relative to the others. This is an important step in making decisions on items like investments, business priorities, and features or requirements—wherever a clear, prioritized list is needed.

NUMBER OF PLAYERS

Small group of 3–10 participants

DURATION OF PLAY

Medium to long; 30 minutes to 1 hour depending on the length of the list, the criteria, and the size of the group

HOW TO PLAY

To set up the game, participants need to have two things: an unranked list of items and the criteria for ranking them. Because forced ranking makes the group judge items closely, the criteria should be as clear as possible. For example, in ranking features for a product, the criteria might be "Most important features for User X." In the case of developing business priorities, the criteria might be "Most potential impact over the next year."

If there are multiple dimensions to a ranking, it is best to rank the items separately for each criterion, and then combine the scores to determine the final ranking. It is difficult for participants to weigh more than one criterion at a time, as in the confusing "Most potential impact over the next year and least amount of effort over the next six months." In this case, it would be best to rank items twice: once by impact and once by effort.

Although there is no hard limit on the number of items to be ranked, in a small-group setting the ideal length of a list is about 10 items. This allows participants to judge items relative to one another without becoming overwhelming. By making the entire list visible on a flip chart or whiteboard, participants will have an easier time ranking a larger list.

To play, create a matrix of items and the criteria. Each participant ranks the items by assigning it a number, with the most important item being #1, the second most important item as #2, and so forth, to the least important item. Because the ranking is "forced," no items can receive equal weight.

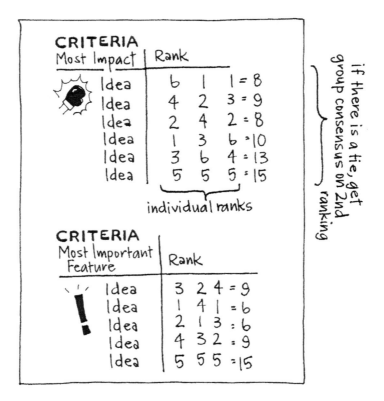

CRITERIA
Most Impact | Rank

	Idea	6	1	1	= 8
	Idea	4	2	3	= 9
	Idea	2	4	2	= 8
	Idea	1	3	6	= 10
	Idea	3	6	4	= 13
	Idea	5	5	5	= 15

individual ranks

CRITERIA
Most Important Feature | Rank

Idea	3	2	4	= 9
Idea	1	4	1	= 6
Idea	2	1	3	= 6
Idea	4	3	2	= 9
Idea	5	5	5	= 15

if there is a tie, get group consensus on 2nd. ranking

Once the items have been ranked, tally them and discuss the prioritized list and next steps.

STRATEGY

Creating a forced ranking may be difficult for participants, as it requires they make clear-cut assessments about a set of items. In many cases, this is not the normal mode of operation for groups, where it is easier to add items to lists to string together agreement and support. Getting people to make these assessments, guided by clear criteria, is the entire point of forced ranking.

The original source of the Forced Ranking game is unknown.

Post-Up

OBJECT OF PLAY

The goal of this game is to generate ideas with silent sticky note writing.

NUMBER OF PLAYERS

1–50

DURATION OF PLAY

10 minutes to 1 hour

HOW TO PLAY

There are many ways to work with ideas using sticky notes. Generating ideas is the most basic play, and it starts with a question that your group will be brainstorming answers to. For example: "What are possible uses for Product X?"

Write the question or topic on a whiteboard. Ask the group to brainstorm answers individually, silently writing their ideas on separate sticky notes. The silence lets people think without interruption, and putting items on separate notes ensures that they can later be shuffled and sorted as distinct thoughts. After a set amount of time, ask the members of the group to stick their notes to the whiteboard and quickly present them.

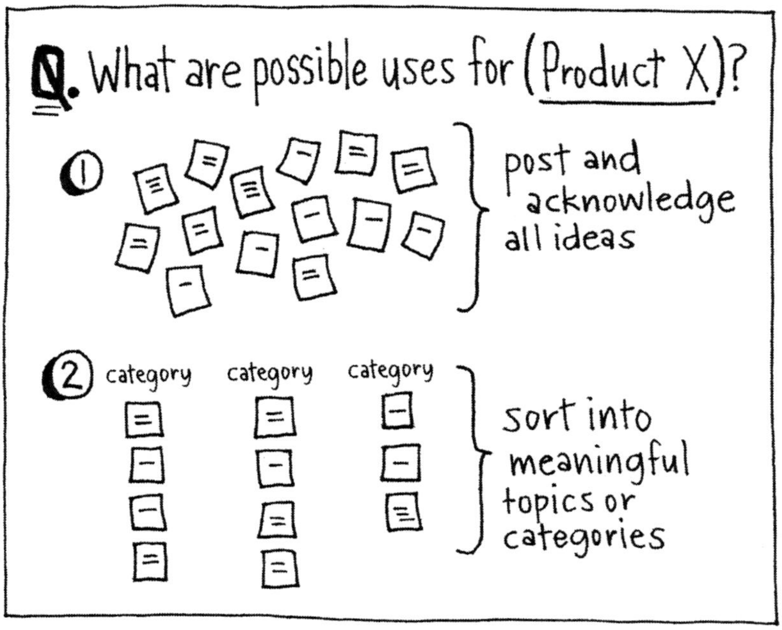

If anyone's items inspire others to write more, they can stick those up on the wall too, after everyone has presented.

STRATEGY

Generating ideas is an opening activity, and a first step. From here you can create an affinity map or a bottom-up tree, or further organize and prioritize the thoughts.

The Post-Up game is based on the exercises in Rapid Problem-Solving with Post-it® Notes *by David Straker.*

Storyboard

OBJECT OF PLAY

This game asks players to envision and describe an ideal future in sequence using words and pictures. Storyboarding as a technique is so versatile that it can be used to show any topic, not just an ideal future. But it is particularly powerful as a visioning exercise since it allows players to imagine and create possibilities. The players tell a story with a happy ending, planting tiny seeds for a different future. You can also use storyboarding to let employees describe their experience on a project, to show approaches to solving a problem, or to orient new employees on policies and procedures—its uses are limited only by the imagination.

NUMBER OF PLAYERS

8–20

DURATION OF PLAY

45 minutes to 1.5 hours

HOW TO PLAY

Before the meeting, determine the topic around which the players will craft their "ideal" story. Once the meeting starts, divide the group into pairs or groups of three or four, depending on the size of the group. Provide markers, pads of flip-chart paper, and stands.

1. Tell the players that the purpose of this game is to tell the other players a feel-good story. The topic of the story is "The Ideal Future for [blank]"—for a team, a product, the company, whatever you decided beforehand. The players' assignment is to visually describe the topic and narrate it to the group.

2. After the groups are established, give them 20–25 minutes to (1) agree on an ideal state, (2) determine what steps they would take to get there, and (3) draw each step as a sequence of large images or scenes, one per sheet of flip-chart paper.

3. Give the players a two-minute time warning, and once the time is up, bring them back together. Ask for volunteers to tell the story first.

4. After all the groups have presented, ask them what's inspiring in what they heard. Summarize any recurring themes and ask for observations, insights, and "aha's" about the stories.

Our Ideal Future State
pow!!
Be the best design studio in the world!
ah ha!
?
dedicated team of researchers
who?
where?
what?
get all resources designers need
HUB
establish active community hub for designers
bits of marketing
attract people to the hub via social tools
1#
SABBY STUDIO
relationships with the best make us the best!

STRATEGY

As the leader of this game, be sensitive to the fact that many of the meeting participants will freak when you tell them that large-scale drawing is involved. Reassure them that the story is the point of the exercise and that the images play a supporting role. They can use words as captions to clarify the images and they can also select the "artist" within their group so that not everyone has to put marker to paper. (But it's more fun for those who do.) Finally, remind them that they aren't allotted sufficient time to create a da Vinci anyway, so stick figures work perfectly well.

For the presentation format, there are various options. Breakout groups can post each sheet of flip-chart paper in a row around the room and walk along the row as they tell the story. They can also leave the flip-chart pad intact and flip the pages over the stand as they narrate. They could choose to hang the sheets in rows and cover them, using one group member to act as a "Vanna White" and create a series of *voilà* moments. Tell them to have fun with it—they aren't being graded on their stories (although you could make it a contest if it's that kind of crowd). The process of creating and sharing the stories is what matters.

Walt Disney is credited for this activity. His need to animate Steamboat Willie *in 1928 led to the process of* storyboarding—*a story told in sequence on a wall covered with a special kind of board. He found it to be an effective way to track progress and improve a story.*

WhoDo

OBJECT OF PLAY
The objective of this game is to brainstorm, plan, and prioritize actions.

NUMBER OF PLAYERS
1–10

DURATION OF PLAY
20–45 minutes

HOW TO PLAY
Who do you want to do what? Almost any endeavor of substantial impact requires seeking help from others. Developing a WHO + DO list is a simple way to scope out the undertaking.

1. Start with the vision. Write out or visualize the big goal.

2. Draw a two-column matrix and write "WHO" on the left and "DO" on the right.

3. Ask: Who is involved in making this happen? Who is the decision maker? Who has needed resources? Who may be an obstacle? Whose support is needed? These individuals or groups are your list of WHOs.

4. The DOs are often harder. For each WHO, ask: What do they need to do, or do differently? What actions will build toward the big goal? Sharpen each WHO in the list until you have a desired and measurable action for each.

WHO + DO	
Sponsors	Donate $5k per program
Board Members	Recommend 3 new sponsors
VP Development	Sign off on event concept
↓...	↓...

Given all of the possible WHOs and DOs, which are the most important? Who comes first?

STRATEGY

Bias yourself toward action. When brainstorming DOs, there is a tendency to slip into the easier mode of "we just want them to understand." Most often when you want people to understand something, it's because you want them to change something or learn something that they can then "DO." Ask yourself, or the group, "What will happen once they understand?" Don't shortchange what you are really looking for: action.

The WhoDo game is credited to Dave Gray.

CHAPTER 5

Games for Opening

OPENING IS TAKING THE FIRST STEP INTO AN EMPTY SPACE. Games that open are focused on framing and describing the bounds of that space and then jumping headfirst into it. In some cases, they foster the spark that produces a large and diverse set of ideas. In other cases, they quickly map out the space in time and scope to be explored.

Some are complete exercises that stand on their own, and others are building blocks that can be composed into larger forms.

When you're facing a blank space, the most difficult mark to make is the first one. Games that open make that mark and serve up the deluge that comes after.

3-12-3 Brainstorm

OBJECT OF PLAY

This format for brainstorming compresses the essentials of an ideation session into one short format. The numbers 3-12-3 refer to the amount of time in minutes given to each of three activities: 3 minutes for generating a pool of observations, 12 for combining those observations into rough concepts, and 3 again for presenting the concepts back to a group.

Essential to this format is strict time keeping. The "ticking clock" forces spontaneous, quick-fire decisions and doesn't allow for overthinking. With this in mind, a group that is typically heavily measured in its thought process will benefit the most from this exercise but will also be the hardest to engage.

Given its short duration (30 minutes total for 10 participants), 3-12-3 Brainstorming can be used as an energizer before diving into a longer exercise or as a standalone, zero-prep activity. It works equally well in generating new ideas as improvements to existing ones.

NUMBER OF PLAYERS

This is a fast exercise that gets slower as more participants are added. With up to 10 participants working as partners, the speed of the exercise makes it an energy builder. Working beyond 10 may require creating groups of three instead of pairs to keep from getting slowed down.

DURATION OF PLAY

21–30 minutes, depending on number of participants

HOW TO PLAY

You will need a topic on which to brainstorm ideas, boiled down to two words. This could be an existing problem, such as "energy efficiency," or it could be focused on creating something new, such as "tomorrow's television."

Although the two words could be presented as a full challenge question, such as "How will tomorrow's television work?" it is best to avoid doing this right away. By focusing on two words that signify the topic, you will aim to evoke thinking about its defining aspects first, before moving into new concepts or proposing solutions.

To set up the game, distribute a stack of index cards and markers to all the participants. Everyone should have a fair number of cards available. The game should begin immediately after the rules have been explained.

3 Minutes: Generate a Pool of Aspects. For the first three minutes of the exercise, participants are asked to think about the characteristics of the topic at hand and to write down as many of them as they can on separate index cards. It may accelerate the group's process to think in terms of "nouns and verbs" that come to mind when thinking about the subject, or to free-associate. As in all brainstorming, no filtering should be put on this phase, in which the goal is a large pool of aspects in a small window of three minutes.

12 Minutes: Develop Concepts. At this point the group is divided into pairs. Each team draws three cards randomly from the pool. With these as thought starters, the teams now have 12 minutes to develop a concept to present back to the larger group.

If the two topic words are sufficient to explain the challenge, the clock starts and the teams begin. If there is any doubt, reveal a more fleshed-out version of the topic's focus, such as "How will we become more energy-efficient next quarter?"

In developing concepts to present, teams may create rough sketches, prototypes, or other media—the key is in preparing for a short (three-minute maximum) presentation of their concept back to the group.

3 Minutes: Make Presentations. When presenting to the larger group, teams may reveal the cards that they drew and how the cards influenced their thinking. Again, tight time keeping is critical here—every team should have a maximum of three minutes to present their concept. After every team has presented, the entire group may reflect on what was uncovered.

STRATEGY

Speed is key. Many traditional brainstorming techniques can be slowed down or fouled entirely when time is not of the essence, despite the best intentions of participants. Additionally, speed helps prove the value of what can be accomplished in short bursts—often the important aspects of good ideas can be captured very quickly and do not require laborious discussion before first coming to light.

After presenting concepts back to the group, teams may do a number of things. They may dig deeper on an individual concept or try to integrate the ideas into each other. They may vote or rank the concepts to decide on which to spend more time developing. Often, concepts coming out of this exercise are more memorable to the participants, who are bonded in the time-driven stress of creating together.

The 3-12-3 Brainstorm game is credited to James Macanufo.

The Anti-Problem

OBJECT OF PLAY

The Anti-Problem game helps people get unstuck when they are at their wit's end. It is most useful when a team is already working on a problem, but they're running out of ideas for solutions. By asking players to identify ways to solve the problem opposite to their current problem, it becomes easier to see where a current solution might be going astray or where an obvious solution isn't being applied.

NUMBER OF PLAYERS

5–20

DURATION OF PLAY

30–45 minutes

HOW TO PLAY

1. Before the meeting, find a situation that needs to be resolved or a problem that needs a solution.

2. Give players access to sticky notes, markers, index cards, pipe cleaners, modeling clay—any supplies you have around the office that they could use to design and describe solutions.

3. Break large groups into smaller groups of three to four people and describe what they'll tackle together: the anti-problem, or the current problem's opposite. (For example, if the problem is sales conversion, the players would brainstorm ways to get customers to avoid buying the product.) The more extreme the problem's opposite, the better.

Optional activity: Bring a list of smaller problems and decrease the amount of time allotted to solve them. Make it a race to come up with as many solutions as the group can churn out—even if they're outlandish.

---

4. Give the players 15–20 minutes to generate and display various ways to solve the anti-problem. Encourage fast responses and a volume of ideas. There are no wrong solutions.

5. When the time is up, ask each group to share their solutions to the anti-problem. They should stand and display any visual creations they have at this time or ask the others to gather around their table to see their solutions.

6. Discuss any insights and discoveries the players have.

STRATEGY

This game's purpose is to help teams evaluate a problem differently and break out of existing patterns, so make the anti-problem more extreme than it really is, just to get people thinking. And don't worry if the players don't generate many (or any) viable or actionable solutions. Obviously, those would be a boon to the game, but the intention is not to eliminate a complex problem in 30 minutes. The intention is to give people a new approach that can lead to a solution when they have time to think after the meeting is over. Or, since this game tends to naturally segue into a conversation about the real problem, you could use any extra time to start that conversation while the players' ideas are ignited. Note: there may be some unexpected "aha moments" as people could discover that they're applying a solution that's actually contributing to the current problem. Whoops!

The Anti-Problem game is based on an activity called Reverse It, *from Donna Spencer's design games website,* http://www.designgames.com.au.

Brainwriting

OBJECT OF PLAY

Some of the best ideas are compilations from multiple contributors. Brainwriting is a simple way to generate ideas, share them, and subsequently build on them within a group. Access to multiple hands, eyes, and minds can yield the most interesting results.

NUMBER OF PLAYERS

5–15

DURATION OF PLAY

30–45 minutes

HOW TO PLAY

1. In a space visible to the players, write the topic around which you need to generate ideas and draw a picture of it. An example of a topic might be "Employee Recognition Program."

2. Distribute index cards to each player and ask them to silently generate ideas related to the topic and write them on the cards.

3. As they complete each idea, ask the players to pass that idea to the person on their right.

4. Tell the players to read the card they received and think of it as an "idea stimulation" card. Ask them to add an idea inspired by what they just read or to enhance the idea and then pass again to their right.

5. Continue this process of "brainwriting" and passing cards to the right until there are various ideas on each card.

Optional activity: Ask the players to write an idea on a piece of paper and then fold it into an airplane and fly it to another participant. Continue writing and flying the planes until each piece of paper has several ideas. Conclude with steps 6 and 7.

---

6. Once finished, collect the cards and ask for help taping them to the wall around the topic and its picture.

7. Have the group come to the wall to review the ideas and draw stars next to the ones they find most compelling. Discuss.

> *Optional activity: Create an idea gallery in the room using flip-chart pads and stands. Ask players to write as many ideas on the sheet as they can and then wander around the room and add ideas to the other sheets. Continue this process until each sheet has a good number of ideas.*

STRATEGY

In a typical group setting, extroverts tend to dominate the verbal contributions. And while their contributions are certainly important, it can be difficult to hear from quieter players who also have something valuable to offer. Let the players know that this play is intentionally silent. It affords the quiet people the opportunity to generate ideas without having to verbalize to the whole group, and it gives you certainty that you'll hear from every player in the room. Brainwriting also allows ideas to emerge *before* being critiqued and creates a space for them to be co-created, with multiple owners, and therefore a greater chance of follow-through.

The Brainwriting game is based on the same-named activity in Michael Michalko's Thinkertoys. *Horst Geschke and associates at the Batelle Institute in Frankfurt, Germany, developed a variety of these creative-thinking techniques referred to as "brainwriting."*

Context Map

OBJECT OF PLAY

We don't truly have a good grasp of a situation until we see it in a fuller context. The Context Map, therefore, is designed to show us the external factors, trends, and forces at work surrounding an organization. Because once we have a systemic view of the external environment we're in, we are better equipped to respond proactively to that landscape.

NUMBER OF PLAYERS

5–25

DURATION OF PLAY

45 minutes to 1.5 hours

HOW TO PLAY

1. Hang six sheets of flip-chart paper on a wall in a two-row, three-column format.

2. On the top-middle sheet of flip-chart paper, draw a representation of the organization under discussion. It can be as simple as an image of your office building or an image of a globe to represent a global marketplace. Label the picture or scene.

3. On the same sheet of paper, above and to the left of the image, write the words "POLITICAL FACTORS". Above and to the right, write the words "ECONOMIC CLIMATE".

4. On the top-left sheet of flip-chart paper, draw several large arrows pointing to the right. Label this sheet "TRENDS". Include a blank before the word *TRENDS* so that you can add a qualifier later.

5. On the top-right sheet of flip-chart paper, draw several large arrows pointing to the left. Label this sheet "TRENDS". Again, include a blank before the word *TRENDS* so that you can add a qualifier later.

6. On the bottom-left sheet, draw large arrows pointing up and to the right. Label this sheet "TECHNOLOGY FACTORS".

7. On the bottom-middle sheet, draw an image representing your client(s) and label the sheet "CUSTOMER NEEDS".

8. On the bottom-right sheet, draw a thundercloud or a person with a question mark overhead and label this sheet "UNCERTAINTIES".

9. Introduce the context map to the group. Explain that the goal of populating the map is to get a sense of the big picture in which your organization operates. Ask the players which category on the map they'd like to discuss first, other than TRENDS. Open up the category they select for comments and discussion. Write the comments they verbalize in the space created for that category.

10. Based on an indication from the group or your own sense of direction, move to another category and ask the group to offer ideas for that category. Continue populating the map with content until every category but TRENDS is filled in.

11. The two TRENDS categories can be qualified by the group, so take a quick poll to determine what kinds of trends the players would like to discuss. These could be online trends, demographic trends, growth trends, and so forth. As you help the players find agreement on qualifiers for the trends (conduct a dot vote or have them raise their hands if you need to), write those qualifiers in the blanks next to TRENDS. Then continue the process of requesting content and writing it in the appropriate space.

12. Summarize the overall findings with the group and ask for observations, insights, "aha's," and concerns about the context map.

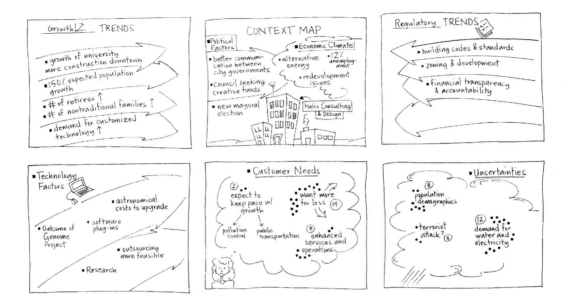

STRATEGY

It's up to the players to paint a picture of the environment in which they sit, but as the meeting leader, you can help them generate content by asking intelligent and thought-provoking questions. Conduct research or employee interviews before the meeting if you need to. The idea is to portray a context that is as rich and accurate as possible so that the players gain insight into their environment and can subsequently move proactively rather than reactively. The players can populate the categories other than TRENDS on the context map in any order, so note their starting point and pay attention to where they focus or generate the most content—both can indicate where their energy lies. But keep in mind that this activity is designed to generate a display of the external environment, not the internal one. So, if you notice that the discussion steers toward analyzing the internal context, guide them back to the outside world. There are other games for internal dynamics. The Context Map game should result in a holistic view of the external business landscape and show the group where they can focus their efforts to get strategic results.

This game is based on The Grove Consultants International's Leader's Guide to Accompany the Context Map Graphic Guide® ©1996–2010 *The Grove.*

Cover Story

OBJECT OF PLAY

Cover Story is a game about pure imagination. The purpose is to think expansively around an ideal future state for the organization; it's an exercise in visioning. The object of the game is to suspend all disbelief and envision a future state that is so stellar that it landed your organization on the cover of a well-known magazine. The players must pretend as though this future has already taken place and has been reported by the mainstream media. This game is worth playing because it not only encourages people to "think big," but also actually plants the seeds for a future that perhaps wasn't possible before the game was played.

NUMBER OF PLAYERS

Any

DURATION OF PLAY

Depends on the number of players, but a maximum of 90 minutes

HOW TO PLAY

1. Before the meeting, draw out large-scale templates that include the categories shown on the following image. Your template doesn't need to look exactly like this one; you can be creative with the central image and the layout. Just be sure to keep the categories intact. The number of templates you create depends on the size of the group. At the most, allow four to six people to work on one template together.

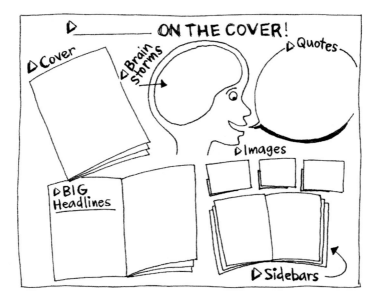

2. Explain the object of the game to the players and define each category on the template:

   - "Cover" tells the BIG story of their success.

   - "Headlines" convey the substance of the cover story.

   - "Sidebars" reveal interesting facets of the cover story.

   - "Quotes" can be from anyone as long as they're related to the story.

   - "Brainstorm" is for documenting initial ideas for the cover story.

   - "Images" are for supporting the content with illustrations.

3. Break the players into groups of four to six and make sure there are markers and one template for each group. Tell the players that to populate the template they can either select a scribe or write and draw on it together.

4. Ask the players to imagine the best-case scenario for their company and to take that scenario one step further. Request that they spend five quiet minutes imagining their own stories before they work together to agree on one. Give the groups 30–45 minutes to generate this "story of the year" and represent it on their template.

5. Reconvene the breakout groups and ask for volunteers to present their visions first. Give each group 5–10 minutes to share what they imagined was written in the story and the supporting elements.

6. Note any common vision themes and areas of agreement. Ask for observations, insights, and concerns about the future state.

Optional activity: Ask two players to role-play an interview based on the content from their "On the Cover" template, as though the magazine sent a reporter to interview an important character in the story.

STRATEGY

This game is about the wildest dream for the organization—that has already happened! So, when you set up this game as the meeting leader, speak about their "successes" with enthusiasm and in the past tense. Encourage the players to use the past tense in their brainstorming and story creation. And don't let the group go into analysis mode. This game is not about logic, pragmatism, or parameters. Cover Story is an open-ended, creative-thinking exercise, so tell the players to be wary of any "reality checks" from other players. And as the small groups present their visions to the large group, note and discuss any common themes that arise. These themes—however fantastical—are telling, because commonalities reveal shared hopes and also plant seeds for real possibilities. If this play is part of a longer group process, post these visions around the room so that they serve as reference points for continued ideas and inspiration.

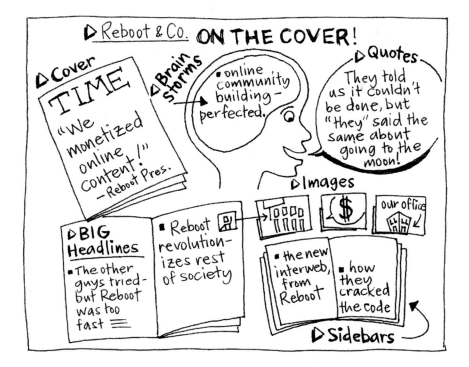

This game is based on The Grove Consultants International's Leaders Guide to Accompany the Cover Story Vision Graphic Guide® ©1996–2010 The Grove.

Draw the Problem

OBJECT OF PLAY

On any given day, we prioritize the problems that get our attention. Problems that are vague or misunderstood have a harder time passing our internal tests of what matters and, as a result, go unaddressed and unsolved. Often, meetings that address problem solving skip this critical step: defining the problem in a way that is not only clear but also compelling enough to make people care about solving it.

Running this short drawing exercise at the beginning of a meeting will help get the laptops closed and the participants engaged with their purpose.

NUMBER OF PLAYERS

Works best with small groups of 6–10 participants

DURATION OF PLAY

20–30 minutes

HOW TO PLAY

Each participant should have a large index card or letter-sized piece of paper. After introducing the topic of the meeting, ask the participants to think about the problem they are here to solve. As they do so, ask them to write a list of items helping to explain the problem. For example, they may think about a "day in the life" of the problem or an item that represents the problem as a whole.

The Problem: Distribution Channel is getting man-handled.

1. service population growing exponentially
2. so is their purchasing power
3. infrastructure changing shape
4. eco-friendly consumer demands
5. rise in micro-markets

(index card front)

After a few minutes of this thinking and reflection, ask the participants to flip over their paper and draw a picture of the problem, as they would explain it to a peer. They may draw a simple diagram or something more metaphorical; there are no prizes or punishments for good or bad artistry. The drawing should simply assist in explaining the problem.

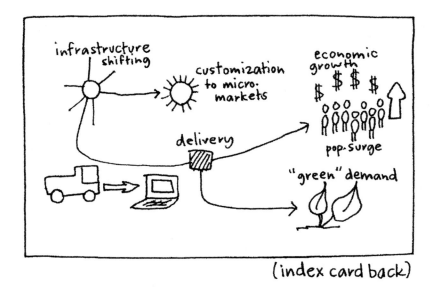

(index card back)

When everyone is finished, have the participants post their drawings on the wall and explain them to each other. While the group shares, note any common elements. After the exercise, the group should reflect on the similarities and differences, and work toward a shared understanding of what the problem looks like to each other.

STRATEGY

This warm-up does not result in a problem definition that will satisfy an engineer; rather, it engages participants in defining the challenge in a simplified form. It is a first step in bringing a group together under a common purpose, elevating the problem above the noise to become something they care to solve.

The Draw the Problem game is credited to James Macanufo.

Fishbowl

OBJECT OF PLAY

Often during meetings we bring together stakeholders who aren't familiar with each other's perspectives or aren't accustomed to listening to each other without offering an immediate response. In some cases, stakeholders may even be meeting for the first time. In scenarios like these, it's not surprising that it can be difficult for people to engage in a rich and meaningful conversation. The Fishbowl game is an effective way to activate attention—to prime our natural listening and observing skills so that a more substantive conversation can take place.

NUMBER OF PLAYERS

Medium to large groups

DURATION OF PLAY

40–45 minutes

HOW TO PLAY

1. Before the meeting, think of a topic that could be served by a group discussion and write down questions associated with it.

2. Find a room with a good amount of open space and clear out anything other than chairs.

3. Create a handout similar to the following:

4. Arrange the chairs in two concentric circles in the room, as shown in the following figure. The inner circle seats the players engaged in conversation; the outer circle seats the players acting as observers.

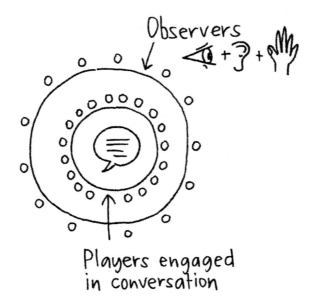

5. Introduce the game and assign "observer" or "player" status to each person. Give everyone a pen and a handout (but mention that the handout is used only in the observer role). Ask the participants to sit in the circle relative to their assigned role.

6. Announce the topic of the game and ask the players to take 15 minutes to have a discussion around it. Use the questions you generated before the meeting to start the conversation and keep it moving. Make sure the players know that their responsibility is simply to converse in the circle. Make sure the observers know that their role is to pay close attention and to write on the handouts all discussion points and evidence that come out of the conversation.

7. When 15 minutes are up, ask the group to switch seats and switch roles. Then start another 15-minute discussion on the same topic or a different one.

8. After both conversations have completed, ask for volunteers to share the information they gathered and ask them to describe their experiences on the inner versus outer circle.

STRATEGY

People are well versed in having conversations; what most of us aren't used to is listening, observing, and being accountable for our observations. The Fishbowl game, therefore, is about engaging skills that in many of us have become rusty. So, despite the fact that it may look as though the action happens in the players' conversation, the action in this game happens in the outer circle, with the observers. As the group leader, be clear with the group that this is a listening and observing exercise. If there were a point system (and there is decidedly not), points would be awarded to those who most accurately logged the conversation that took place—not to those who made the most comments in the discussion. Talk to the group about their experience of being silent and paying attention. What was difficult about it? What was easy? How did it affect their perception of the topic and the other players? Use the Fishbowl exercise as a segue to a heightened give-and-take between stakeholders.

The Fishbowl game is based on ideas from the Facilitator's Guide to Participatory Decision-Making, *by Sam Kaner et al.*

Forced Analogy

OBJECT OF PLAY

We understand things by grouping them with other things of similar type and function. An airplane is similar to a helicopter; they're both flying things. Both are more similar to a bird, which is also a flying thing, than any of those things are to an earthworm, which is a crawling and tunneling thing. The Forced Analogy game breaks these hard-wired categories and allows us to see things from a different angle, opening new possibilities in problem solving and idea generation.

NUMBER OF PLAYERS

1–10

DURATION OF PLAY

15 minutes to 1 hour

HOW TO PLAY

Participants set up the exercise by generating a random list of things—animals, objects, or people. Write these items on individual index cards. For each item, write some of its qualities or attributes—for example, "An airplane flies through the air, moves along pre-defined routes, and has an autopilot feature." Likewise, an oak tree would be noted for its branching structure, its deep roots, and its ability to grow from a very small seed.

Participants shuffle the cards and distribute them randomly. They then use the cards to develop analogies to the problem or issue at hand, asking:

- How is this problem similar to [random object]?
- How would I solve this problem with [random object]?

Participants may also work through one analogy as a group, as in "How would we use a paperclip to solve our data integration problem?"

STRATEGY

A truly random list of objects will push the boundaries of the group's mindset and create new perspectives. If needed, this list can be created in advance of the game itself by an unbiased nonparticipant.

The source of the Forced Analogy game is unknown.

Graphic Jam

OBJECT OF PLAY

Words become more challenging to visualize as they become less literal. For example, the words *computer* and *necktie* offer immediate imagery. But the words *strategy* and *justice* are more abstract and lend themselves to broader visual interpretations. Graphic Jam is an all-purpose visualization game that you can conduct before many other games as a warm-up, but it's also a useful game in itself. Visualizing abstract concepts supports logo development, presentation design, website design, metaphor development for e-learning, and so on. It exercises the visual part of our cortex—which accounts for 75% of our sensory neurons—and turns on parts of our minds that don't get much action in a typical business setting. Why does that matter? Because business is getting more complex. Being able to use your mind's eye to see and show problems—and solutions—will be a sought-after skill.

NUMBER OF PLAYERS

5–15

DURATION OF PLAY

30 minutes to 1 hour

HOW TO PLAY

1. Establish a large, flat, white display area for this game. Give all players access to sticky notes and index cards.

2. Ask them to take 1–2 minutes to write words *on the index cards* that they have difficulty conceptualizing and drawing, like "quality" or "teamwork." Ask for one word or phrase per index card.

3. Gather all of the contributions, shuffle them, and then draw one card and read it aloud to the group. Tape it up in the white space.

4. Ask the players to reflect on the word and draw a visual representation of it *on a sticky note* so that it can be posted on the wall. Give them 2–3 minutes to do so.

5. Have the players approach the white space and post their sticky note under the index card with the related word.

6. Repeat steps 3–5 until all or most of the words have been read aloud. If you draw repeat words or synonyms of previously drawn words, draw again until you get a fresh concept.

7. By the end of the game, you'll have a gallery space of visualized concepts. Ask the group to spend time looking at how others interpreted the words.

8. Referring to the sticky notes, lead a group discussion by asking what certain images mean and how the artist related that image to the word that was read aloud. Ask players to discuss which words were easier to visualize than others and why. Close by asking them how they might see visualization skills applied in their daily life and work.

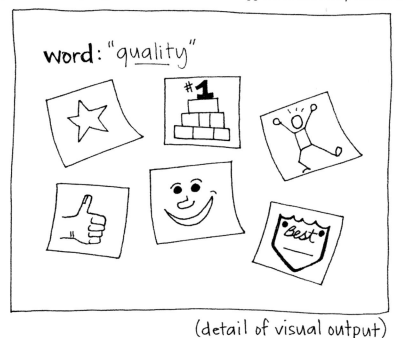

(detail of visual output)

STRATEGY

It is highly likely that the words the players contribute to this game will be on the abstract end of the spectrum. Note that the amount of time you'll need for this game depends on the number of players, the number of words each player generates, and the complexity of the word concepts. Use your best judgment on how long to spend conducting a Graphic Jam session. And when you decide it's time to call it quits, ask the group if there are any burning concepts they'd like to see visualized. If so, take a few more minutes with the group to tackle them. When the game is over, give the players a chance to converse with each other about the creative processes and techniques they use to conjure ideas and imagery.

And one important note: The pace of the Graphic Jam can be ramped up by putting a shorter time limit on how long players have to draw their representations of the words. Give players 30 seconds with a hard stop for each word and you'll see how high the energy level in the room rises. It's not really a competition, but people respond to it that way, and the 30-second round can deliver peak (or at least hilarious!) results.

The Graphic Jam game inspired by the same-named activity created by Leslie Salmon-Zhu, co-founder of the International Forum of Visual Practitioners.

Heuristic Ideation Technique

OBJECT OF PLAY

In this simple game, participants use a matrix to generate new ideas or approaches to a solution. The game gets its name from three heuristics—or rules of thumb—of idea generation:

- A new idea can be generated from remixing the attributes of an existing idea.

- A new idea is best understood by describing its two essential attributes.

- The more different or surprising the combination of the two attributes, the more compelling the idea.

NUMBER OF PLAYERS

1–10

DURATION OF PLAY

15 minutes to 2 hours

HOW TO PLAY

To set up the game, participants decide on two categories of attributes that will define their matrix. For example, a toy manufacturer might look at its product line by type (vehicles, figures and dolls, puzzles, and instruments) and by type of play (racing, simulation, construction). Participants use these lists to populate a matrix, creating a grid of new possible combinations.

TOY IDEAS	Vehicles	Dolls	Puzzles	Instruments
Racing	Slot cars	Wind·up	Speed Puzzle	???
Simulation	Flight Simulator	Voodoo Doll ??	???	"Join the Band"
Construction	Model Kit	Paintable	3·D	Build-an-Instrument

In playing the game, participants look across the cells for unusual or surprising combinations. These become the seeds of new ideas.

STRATEGY

Some combinations that at first seem absurd are worth examining more closely: a toy that combines puzzle pieces with a racing element might seem counterintuitive, but there are classic games built around that principle. After looking across the matrix for such combinations, a group may then develop fast prototypes or sketches that explore the possibilities. Consider that GI-Joe came to life conceptually as a "doll for boys."

The technique used in this game was documented by Edward Tauber in his 1972 paper, "HIT: Heuristic Ideation Technique, A Systematic Procedure for New Product Search."

History Map

OBJECT OF PLAY

Organizations naturally look ahead to anticipate progress. But the past can be as informative as the future. When an organization undergoes systemic or cultural change, documenting its history becomes an important process. By collecting and visualizing the components of history, we necessarily discover, recognize, and appreciate what got us where we are today. We can see the past as a guiding light or a course correction for our future. The History Map game shows you how to map moments and metrics that shaped your organization. It's also a great way to familiarize new people with an organization's history and culture during periods of rapid growth

NUMBER OF PLAYERS

10–50

DURATION OF PLAY

30 minutes to 1.5 hours

HOW TO PLAY

1. Using flip-chart paper and markers, draw a continuous timeline along the bottom of several pages. Hang the paper end to end along a wall. Write the years under the timeline and include an appropriate starting point—don't go back 75 years if you don't need to. Choose a longer time increment, 5- or 10-year windows, if your organization has a long history, and be sure to leave enough space in between years for writing, drawing, and posting content. Leave extra space for years that you know people have more knowledge of or that were years of significant growth or change in the organization.

2. Ask each player to write his name and draw a self-portrait on a sticky note and post it on the wall above the year he joined the organization. As the participants approach the wall for post-ups, ask questions and encourage storytelling about first impressions of the company or why they joined. Note when you see "old-timers" approaching the wall. The richness of their experience can educate the group, so be sure to request that they share a story. Old-timers: never map a history without them.

Optional activity: Before they post the sticky notes, ask the group to stand up and form a line based on when they joined the organization. Let them discover who came on board when and let the line self-organize based on these discovery conversations. Ask for their thoughts and observations once the line is sorted.

3. Ask questions to the group about the following, and build the history map by plotting their answers using text and images:

- Company successes
- Lessons learned
- Changes in leadership and vision
- Culture shifts
- Trends in the marketplace
- Structural reorganizations
- The ebb and flow of regulations
- Shifts in revenue and number of employees
- Major projects, etc.

4. If you're not comfortable drawing improvisationally, establish icons before the meeting to categorize events for easy visual recognition. (For example, you can use stars for successes, arrows for increases or decreases in revenue or employees, a toolbox for projects, etc.) As you add content, refer to items you're adding and ask open-ended questions about them to keep the conversation going.

5. Summarize the findings and ask the players what they learned and why they believe the history of an organization is important. Look for emergent patterns in the life of the organization and verbally relate the history to the future. Request the thoughts, feelings, and observations of the players.

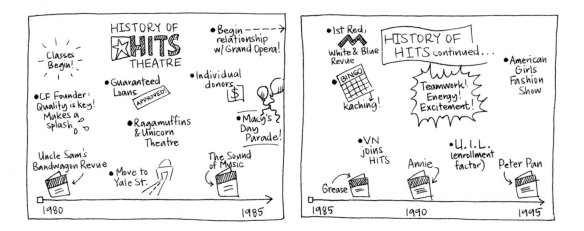

(The History Map continues on the next page)

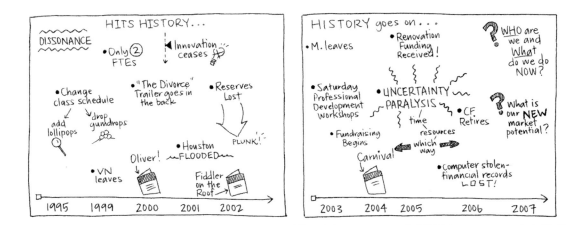

STRATEGY

Mapping a history should be an enjoyable experience for the meeting leader and the participants. It's a time for storytelling, reflection, and appreciation of the life and experience of the organization. While you're helping the group document the history, set a supportive tone and encourage camaraderie, storytelling, and honesty—even about the hard times. And if the meeting runs relatively long, leave the history map posted so that the players can review it during a break and continue to breathe life into it. Let the story build even when you're not conducting the story session. To make the creation of the map logistically easier for you as the meeting leader, follow these tips:

- Always be aware of the level of institutional memory in the meeting. If you're running a game that would work better with experienced employees, include them. If you're running a game that would work better with new eyes and fresh ideas, include newer employees. Pay attention to the knowledge and experience level of the players as it relates to your desired outcome. Brand the history map with the company's logo and write a phrase beforehand that sums up the current vision and culture.

- Draw major events on the map beforehand to use as conversation starters.

- Use sticky notes for events where people are unsure of the dates or metrics so that you can log more accurate information later.

The History Map game is based on The Grove Consultants International's Leader's Guide to Accompany the Graphic History Graphic Guide® ©1996–2010 The Grove.

Image-ination

OBJECT OF PLAY

To generate new ideas about a topic you feel stuck on.

NUMBER OF PLAYERS

5–7 per group

DURATION OF PLAY

15 minutes–1 hour

HOW TO PLAY:

1. Before the meeting, assemble a collection of photographs and images that do not contain words. You can cut them out of magazines, catalogs, or junk mail. Don't look for pretty pictures; instead look for the widest variety of pictures. Try to collect 3–5 pictures per person.

2. Put a large sheet of paper on the table; a piece of flip-chart paper is ideal. In the center, write out a one- to three-word description of the topic you want to generate new thinking around (e.g., Finding New Customers).

3. Place the pictures face down around the edges of the paper. Give each person a pile of sticky notes or index cards.

4. Tell the participants that the goal of the game is to encourage thinking as widely as possible. The idea is to go beyond what they already know. Demonstrate this by showing an image and quickly state several ways it relates to the topic.

5. Have each participant randomly select an image, turn it over, and write on the sticky notes or index cards as many ideas as they can come up with about how the image relates or could relate to the topic. Ask each participant to put one idea on each note or card and put it on the flip-chart paper around the topic.

6. Allow five minutes for participants to work silently. Have people select other images and repeat the process until you either run out of images or time.

7. Ask the group to collect the notes and cards with all of the ideas and re-arrange the ideas in clusters that relate to each other. For each cluster, ask the group to find a photograph to illustrate the idea and create a short title for it. Write the title under the image.

8. If you have more than one small group, ask each one to share the photos and titles of each of their clusters with the other groups.

9. Talk about how the titled photos can inform the groups' thinking about the topic. Make a list of possible actions they could take in response to the ideas.

STRATEGY

Images have the ability to spark insights and to create new associations and possible connections. Encourage people to free-associate and see potential new ideas. In this type of play, you are asking people to move back and forth between using their visual and verbal skills. When done in rapid succession, as in this game, this switching offers the possibility for more ideas and approaches to emerge.

When leading the game, some participants may need to be reassured that the goal is not to come up with a design or specific answer. Keeping the timeframes short reduces this impulse and requires people to allow associations to emerge from a less-considered space. After all, if what everyone was already thinking could readily solve the problem, the group would not feel stuck. The idea is to move beyond the stories people always tell and to surface something new and different.

You may hear that people can't find the picture they want to describe their ideas. That's actually a good sign! That "problem" actually means the participants have the creative opportunity to find another kind of association.

The Image-ination game is based on Picture This! adapted from the Visual Icebreaker Kit, one of several image-based games and tools from VisualsSpeak. It is © 2010 VisualsSpeak LLC.

Low-Tech Social Network

OBJECT OF PLAY

The object of this game is to introduce event participants to each other by co-creating a mural-sized, visual network of their connections.

NUMBER OF PLAYERS

Large groups in an event setting

DURATION OF PLAY

25 minutes to create the first version of the network; the network remains up for the duration of the event, and may be added to, changed, or studied throughout

HOW TO PLAY

To set up the game, all participants will need a 5×8 index card and access to markers or something similar to draw their avatar. They will also need a substantial wall covered in butcher paper to create the actual network.

1. An emcee or leader for the event gives the participants clear instructions: "As a group, we are going to build the social network that is in the room right now. We're going to use this wall to do it. But first, we need to create the most fundamental elements of the network: who you are. Start by taking your card and drawing your avatar (profile picture) that you'll be uploading to the network. Save room on the bottom of the card for your name."

2. **Create the avatars.** After a short period of time (and probably some laughter and apologies for drawing ability), the participants should have their avatars and names created. At this point, the emcee may add a variation, which is to ask the group to also write two words on the card that "tag" who they are or what they're interested in at the event.

3. **Make the connections.** Next, the emcee directs participants to stand up and bring their cards and a marker to the butcher paper wall, then "upload" themselves by sticking their card to the wall.

4. The next task is simple: find the people you know and draw lines to make the connections. Label the lines if you can: "friends with" or "went to school with" or "went mountain climbing with." This continues for a time and is likely to result in previously undiscovered links and new friends.

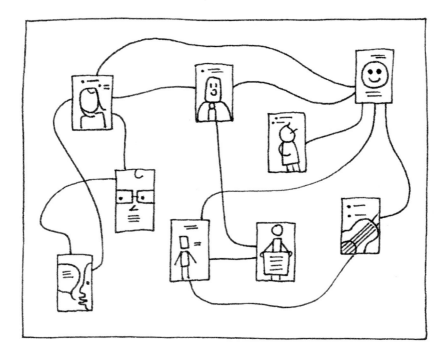

STRATEGY

The initial network creation will be somewhat chaotic and messy, resulting in a mural that has a lot of spaghetti lines. Over the course of the event, participants may browse the network. Encourage this, and see what new connections are made.

The source of Low-Tech Social Network is unknown.

Mission Impossible

OBJECT OF PLAY

To truly create something new, we must challenge constraints. In this exercise, participants take an existing design, process, or idea and change one foundational aspect that makes it "impossible" in function or feasibility. For example:

- "How do we build a house...in a day?"

- "How do we create a mobile device...with no battery?"

- "What would a browser be...without an Internet connection?"

NUMBER OF PLAYERS

Small groups

DURATION OF PLAY

45 minutes to 1 hour, depending on the size of the group

HOW TO PLAY

When a problem is interesting and important, we naturally rise to the occasion. To set up the exercise, develop a question in advance that engages both the emotional and the rational parts of the brain. A mobile device without batteries would be an engineering feat (rational) and a make-the-world-better proposition (emotional). Write this question for the group and explain the challenge.

For the next 30 minutes, working in pairs or small teams, the groups develop approaches to accomplishing the "impossible." They may consider these broad questions or develop a set that is more specific to the challenge:

- What new benefits or features might emerge from this constraint?

- Why is this a typical constraint or requirement? Is it just a customary assumption?

- What are the core elements in conflict?

- Can the conflicting elements be eliminated, replaced, or altered in some way?

- Is there anything that can happen before or after to change the parts in conflict?

- Can time, space, materials, motion, or the environment have an effect?

At the end of the 30 minutes, groups present their concepts to each other. Following this, a reflective discussion about both common and uncommon approaches should yield a list of possible solutions to be explored further. Closing and next steps should include this follow-up work.

STRATEGY

This challenge works well for thinking through assumptions and obstacles in a product or a process. When a product is languishing and needs to be reimagined, this technique will help challenge basic assumptions about its design. In cases where processes are slow or overloaded, the "fire drill" question of "How would we do this in a day?" can be a powerful framing device.

The Mission Impossible game is credited to James Macanufo.

Object Brainstorm

OBJECT OF PLAY

Objects play a special role in brainstorming. A tangible object helps externalize the thought process, just as sketching or role play does, but often in a more immediate and concrete way. Because objects suggest stories about how they might be used, they make a great starting point for free association and exploration.

NUMBER OF PLAYERS

Any

DURATION OF PLAY

30 minutes or more

HOW TO PLAY

Before you can play, you will need to hunt down a collection of objects. Nominate yourself as the curator of your collection. It's worth considering what kind of investment you want to make. Although a trip to a second-hand store to find interesting (and cheap) items is a good start, if you are expecting to make a habit out of the exercise it may be worth the time and expense to look for items more broadly.

Although you will find your own criteria for your collection, one rule of thumb is to collect "things that do things." Functional objects can offer more inspiration. Other things may make it into the collection based on their characteristics or personality, or simply because they are "fun." Here are some types of objects to consider collecting:

- Kitchen gadgets
- Hand tools
- Instruction manuals
- Functional packaging and dispensers
- Containers and compartments
- Sports equipment
- Toys and games

A good collection will evolve over time, and a good curator will get others involved in contributing to the cache of items.

Object brainstorming starts with a question, such as "How will the next generation of [fill-in-the-blank] work?" This question may ask participants to reimagine an existing product or invent something new.

1. Direct the group to explore the objects and to take some time to play with them. The objects may inspire participants to think about how a new thing could function, or how it could look or feel. The long, hinged mouth of a stapler may suggest a new way to bend and fasten steel. A telescoping curtain rod might inspire thinking about a collapsible bicycle. Likewise, an object's personality, such as a rugged toolbox, might suggest how a laptop might be designed. Most objects explain themselves, and the results can be very intuitive; participants are likely to stumble on fully formed ideas.

2. After a set amount of time, the participants share their ideas, document them, and decide on next steps. This may be as simple as voting on an idea to pursue in more detail, or it may mean moving into another brainstorming exercise.

STRATEGY

One choice to make before an object brainstorm is whether to use a set of items or a single item. This changes the depth of focus: a group presented with a set will branch into a wider path of ideas, whereas a group presented with one item is "forced" into a deeper study of the object and associations from it, along the lines of random inputs or forced analogy. Try to use a set of items for larger groups and more divergent brainstorming, and a single item for smaller groups and more focused inquiry.

The source for the Object Brainstorm game is unknown.

Pecha Kucha/Ignite

OBJECT OF PLAY

These fast, structured talks enable people to share ideas quickly and with a minimum of distraction. In addition, it puts the pressure on the person conveying the information to do so in a concise and compelling fashion.

NUMBER OF PLAYERS

Any size, from a small working group to an auditorium full of people.

DURATION OF PLAY

Can go anywhere from one to four hours. Total time varies widely based on the number of presenters.

HOW TO PLAY

Pecha Kucha is based on a simple idea: that by limiting the number of slides in a presentation, and limiting the amount of time a presenter can spend on each slide, presentations will convey information concisely and at a rapid pace. The rule of Pecha Kucha is 20 x 20: Presenters are allowed 20 slides, and they can spend 20 seconds per slide. Images are forwarded automatically—they are not under the control of the speaker. Another variation, Ignite, has a similarly structured pace.

By tradition, Pecha Kucha and Ignite nights are fun, informal evening events, but the concept will work just as well within any work group or team.

STRATEGY

The goal of these talks is to constrain presenters while keeping things fun. Often drinks and snacks are involved, and the right emcee can make a big difference in the quality of the experience. If you have a lot of people, spend some time on details, like picking a venue with good acoustic qualities and arranging for good sound and video equipment. Make sure not to give presenters control of their laptops!

Pecha Kucha (pronounced peh-CHA kuh-CHA—Japanese for "chit chat") began as an event in Tokyo where designers could share their ideas. The Pecha Kucha presentation format was devised by Astrid Klein and Mark Dytham of Klein Dytham architecture. The first Pecha Kucha Night was held in Tokyo in their gallery, lounge, bar, club, and creative kitchen Super-Deluxe in February 2003. Since then, Pecha Kucha has inspired similar events with some minor variations, including Talk20 (short presentations of 20 slides each) and Ignite (short presentations of 20 slides each, 15 seconds per slide).

Pie Chart Agenda

OBJECT OF PLAY

Many meetings happen in an ad hoc or moment-to-moment fashion. They happen without a formal plan, agenda, or prep work—but despite this they can be some of the most productive meetings we have. One characteristic that sets these meetings apart is a focused awareness of time constraints—for example, "We have 30 minutes; how should we spend the time?"

Sketching a pie chart agenda answers this question with speed and clarity. In some cases it takes less than a minute, and in the process, it brings into focus both the order and the significance of topics, where a simple list would fall short. What a pie chart agenda lacks in formality it makes up for in speed and flexibility.

NUMBER OF PLAYERS

Small group

DURATION OF PLAY

60–90 seconds

HOW TO PLAY

1. Draw a circle representing your "pie" of time. This may be on a whiteboard, a flip chart, or even a pad of paper. This circle represents the total amount of time the group has to spend on the objective.

2. Write the objective in the middle of the circle. For instance, it could be "Brainstorm approaches for dealing with Problem X."

3. The group then thinks about how they want to spend the time and adds these items to the clock in a sequence that makes sense for the task at hand, just as they would for a circle-formatted agenda. These are added around the outside.

4. To finish the chart, the group decides how much time they want to reserve for each item. This is captured on the pie chart, as though it were rough sections of a clock face. For instance: "We're going to spend a third of our time on this item, but we need to save the bulk of it for this, and the last five minutes talking about this."

5. Once the group has roughed in the plan and is in agreement, the clock starts ticking and the meeting begins.

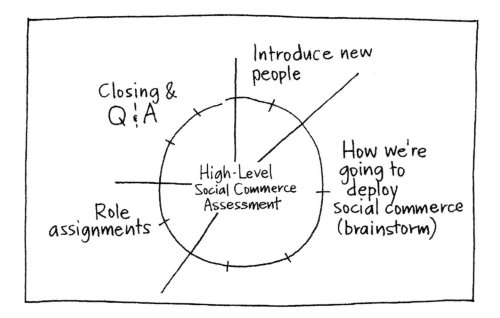

STRATEGY

How is this different from a list agenda? The focal point of a clock does two things. As a metaphor, it emphasizes the notion of time and expediency, which is vital in making ad hoc meetings productive. It also represents the agenda items as parts of the whole, weighted by importance and time to be spent on them. Items on a list have a bad habit of falling off the list or being skipped entirely. When produced quickly and managed through the course of a meeting, a clock agenda helps ensure that the time is spent wisely.

The Pie Chart Agenda is credited to James Macanufo.

Poster Session

OBJECT OF PLAY

If a picture is worth a thousand words, what would 50 pictures be worth? What if 50 people could present their most passionate ideas to each other—without any long-winded explanation? A poster session accelerates the presentation format by breaking it down, forcing experts to boil up their ideas and then present back to each other via simple images.

NUMBER OF PLAYERS

10–100

DURATION OF PLAY

20 minutes to develop posters, an unlimited time to browse

HOW TO PLAY

The goal of a poster session is to create a set of compelling images that summarize a challenge or topic for further discussion. Creating this set might be an "opening act" which then sets the stage for choosing an idea to pursue, or it might be a way to get indexed on a large topic. The act of creating a poster forces experts and otherwise passionate people to stop and think about the best way to communicate the core concepts of their material, avoiding the popular and default "show up and throw up."

To set up, everyone will need ample supplies for creating their poster. Flip charts and markers are sufficient, but consider bringing other school supplies to bear: stickers, magazines for cutting up, and physical objects.

Start the game play by first framing the challenge. In any given large group, you could say the following: "There are more good ideas in everyone's heads than there is time to understand and address them. By creating posters that explain the ideas, we'll have a better idea of what's out there and what we might work on."

The participants' task is to create a poster that explains their topic. There are two constraints:

It must be self-explanatory. If you gave it to a person without walking her through it, would she understand?

It must be visual. Words and labels are good, but text alone will not be enough to get people's attention, or help them understand.

When creating their poster, participants may be helped by thinking about three kinds of explanation:

Before and After: Describe "why" someone should care in terms of drawing the today and tomorrow of the idea.

System: Describe the "what" of an idea in terms of its parts and their relationships.

Process: Describe the "how" of an idea in terms of a sequence of events.

Give participants 20 minutes to create their posters. When they have finished, create a "gallery" of the images by posting them on the wall.

Instead of elaborate presentations, ask the group to circulate and walk the gallery. Some posters will attract and capture more attention than others. From here, it may be worthwhile to have participants dot vote (see Dot Voting in Chapter 4) or "vote with their feet" to decide what ideas to pursue further.

STRATEGY

As a variation, the posters may be created in small groups. In this case, it's important for the group to have decided ahead of time what their topic will be, and to give more time to come to a consensus on what they will draw and how they will draw it.

On a smaller scale, a group may do this around a conference table. A small group of experts may create posters to explain their different points of view to each other at the start of a meeting, to make their models of the world, their vocabulary, and their interests clear and explicit. Twenty minutes spent in this way may save the group from endless discussion later in their process.

The Poster Session game is based on academic poster sessions, in which authors of papers that are not ready for publication share their ideas in an informal, conversational group.

Pre-Mortem

OBJECT OF PLAY

Often in projects, the learning is all at the wrong end. Usually after things have already gone horribly wrong or off-track, members of the team gather in a "postmortem" to sagely reflect on what bad assumptions and courses of action added up to disaster. What makes this doubly unfortunate is that those same team members, somewhere in their collective experience, may have seen it coming.

A pre-mortem is a way to open a space in a project at its inception to directly address its risks. Unlike a more formal risk analysis, the pre-mortem asks team members to directly tap into their experience and intuition, at a time when it is needed most, and is potentially the most useful.

NUMBER OF PLAYERS

Any, but typically small teams will have the most open dialogue

DURATION OF PLAY

Depends on the scope of an effort; allow up to five minutes for each participant

HOW TO PLAY

A pre-mortem is best conducted at the project's kickoff, with all key team members present and after the goals and plan have been laid out and understood. The exercise starts with a simple question: "What will go wrong?" though it may be elevated in phrasing to "How will this end in disaster?"

This is an opportunity for the team to reflect on their collective experience and directly name risks or elephants lurking in the room. It's a chance to voice concerns that might otherwise go unaddressed until it's too late. A simple discussion may be enough to surface these items among a small team; in a larger group, Post-Up or list generation may be needed.

To close the exercise, the list of concerns and risks may be ranked or voted on to determine priority. The group then decides what actions need to be taken to address these risks; they may bring these up as a part of ongoing meetings as the project progresses.

STRATEGY

Conducting a pre-mortem is deceptively simple. At the beginning of a project, the forward momentum and enthusiasm are often at their highest; these conditions do not naturally lend themselves to sharing notions of failure. By conducting a pre-mortem, a group deliberately creates a space to share their past learning, at a time when they can best act on it.

The Pre-Mortem game is credited to James Macanufo.

Show and Tell

OBJECT OF PLAY

You may remember Show and Tell from kindergarten—kids bring their favorite thing to school and tell the class what it means to them. Well, there's more intelligence in that activity than you may have realized. Meeting leaders can conduct Show and Tell to get a better understanding of stakeholders' perspectives on any topic—a project, a restructuring, a shift in the company's vision, a product, and so forth. Show and Tell lets employees use objects for storytelling around things that are important to the organization.

NUMBER OF PLAYERS

5–15

DURATION OF PLAY

20–45 minutes

HOW TO PLAY

1. A few days in advance of a meeting, ask the players to bring an artifact for Show and Tell. The instructions are to bring something that from their perspective represents the topic that'll be discussed at the meeting. If possible, tell them to keep the item hidden until it's their turn to show it.

2. In a white space visible to all the players, write the topic for this play and draw a picture of it. You can do this beforehand if you prefer. When everyone is assembled with their show piece, ask for volunteers to go first.

3. Pay attention to each player's explanation of why she thought an item represented or reminded her of the topic. Listen for how the item is similar to or different from the topic, and listen for emotive descriptions of the item. Write each contribution in the available white space, and if you can, draw a simple visual of the show piece the person brought next to her comments.

4. Summarize what you've captured and let the group absorb any shared themes of excitement, doubt, or concern. Ask follow-up questions about the content to generate further conversation.

> *Optional activity: Assign a player to be the show photographer. Take snapshots of each person telling his story and create a collage of the images afterward. Hang it in a communal space in the office for continued storytelling, especially if this is a topic that you want the players to continue talking about.*

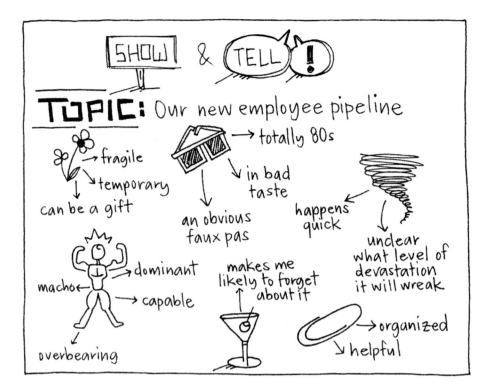

STRATEGY

Show and Tell taps into the power of metaphors to let players share their assumptions and associations around a topic. If you see multiple show pieces that don't exactly represent delight around a topic, that's a signal that the players may have some concerns that need to be addressed. Don't overanalyze the objects; pay more attention to the way the players describe the parallels to the topic. As the team leader, encourage and applaud honesty during the stories, and write down every point that players make that seem important to them. Keep the rest of the players quiet while someone is showing and telling.

For your part, if you feel intimidated by drawing a representation of a player's item in the white space, get through it: attempt to draw it anyway and let the group tease you about your efforts. Show and Tell can be a vulnerable activity for the players—particularly the introverted players—so show some team spirit by being vulnerable yourself.

The Show and Tell game is inspired by the well-known grade school exercise.

Show Me Your Values

OBJECT OF PLAY

Employees' perceptions of a company's values, whether they're conscious or not, contributes to their morale and their willingness to go the extra mile to support the mission. To get a sense of how employees perceive the values that drive an organization, an initiative, a system-wide change, or any other topic, play Show Me Your Values.

NUMBER OF PLAYERS

5–15

DURATION OF PLAY

30–45 minutes

HOW TO PLAY

1. Before the meeting, decide on the topic around which you want players to share stories. Set up a flat surface area on which you can write and they can post their images. Write the name of the topic in this area. Provide the players with tape and several magazines of all genres—enough magazines for each player to rifle through three or four.

2. Tell the players that the goal of the exercise is twofold. First, they'll describe in pictures what they perceive to be the values underlying the topic. Next, they'll share a work-related story that's indicative of those values. (For example, an image of a turtle may represent patience and longevity, so the player may share an anecdote in which an attractive but high-risk project was not pursued.) Most importantly, when you introduce this game, encourage people to share the values they perceive as honestly as they can. Tell them that it's OK to believe that an underlying organizational value is territoriality and to represent that with an image of a lion. Not only is this behavior appropriate, but it's also desirable—since beliefs that drive behavior often go unstated in public but are repeated and spread through huddles within the organization.

3. Give the players 10 minutes to cut out one or more images that represent their perception of the underlying values. Realize that some players will think immediately of a value representing a topic and will hunt through the magazines until they find a suitable representation. Others will surf the images, looking for something that resonates with a vague notion they have in their minds. Either approach is suitable.

Optional activity: Ask the players to cut out images that represent what the values are not. So, if a player believes expediency is not one of the values around a project, she may choose the aforementioned turtle as a representative image.

4. Ask the players to tape their image(s) in the designated area and then quietly reflect on a story associated with the value(s) they represented.

5. Next, ask for volunteers to take turns sharing both their images and their associated story. As people share, if someone expresses difficulty in thinking of a story to match his image, give him more time (or let him bow out completely) and let someone else offer a story related to her image.

6. Pay attention as the players describe the values they perceive and write them in the space next to the appropriate image.

7. Go over the values you captured and ask the players to look for overlaps and gaps in their perception. Ask follow-up questions about the content and stories to generate further conversation. Let the group absorb and discuss the perceptions they share as well as those they don't.

STRATEGY

A notable benefit of using pictures to elicit value statements and stories is that imagery is simultaneously one step removed from a straight, verbal declaration, yet one step deeper than what you may get when you ask players to share their "intellectual" thoughts. And using pictures gives the players a sort of comfort zone in which to express themselves, since they can choose pictures that represent the entire spectrum of comedy and tragedy around a topic.

So, if someone prefers truth through humor, she can find images that allow her to use it. And if someone else prefers truth through hyperbole, well, he has that option too. Let people be creative during the storytelling section of the game. If two or more participants want to share a story together, encourage them to do so. They can even go so far as to role-play an event that unfolded. Your job is to create a space in which people can say something that may be taboo but that *everyone* is thinking.

The Show Me Your Values game is credited to Sunni Brown.

Stakeholder Analysis

OBJECT OF PLAY

The concept of a "stakeholder" has deep roots in business and managerial science, appearing as early as the 18th century in reference to any holder of a bet or wager in an endeavor. The term now has come to mean anyone who can significantly impact a decision, or who may be impacted by it. At the beginning of projects big and small, it may benefit a team to conduct a stakeholder analysis to map out who their stakeholders are—so that they can develop a strategy for engaging them.

NUMBER OF PLAYERS

Any; key members of a team who have a collective awareness of all aspects of a project

DURATION OF PLAY

30 minutes to 1 hour, depending on the depth of the analysis

HOW TO PLAY

There are a number of variations in mapping out stakeholders, and a team may change or add variables to the equation, depending on the circumstances.

The most common way to map is by power and interest.

>**Power:** describes a stakeholder's level of influence in the system—how much he can direct or coerce a project and other stakeholders.

>**Interest:** describes the degree to which a stakeholder will be affected by the project.

By setting up a matrix with these two axes, you are ready to begin.

Step 1: Create a List of Stakeholder Groups

If you do not already have a list of the stakeholders, now is the time to generate it. By using Post-Up or a similar method, create your set of stakeholders by answering these questions:

- Who will be impacted by the project?
- Who will be responsible or accountable for the project?
- Who will have decision authority on the project?
- Who can support the project?
- Who can obstruct the project?
- Who has been involved in this type of project in the past?

A typical list of stakeholders may include these groups:

- The customer, user, or beneficiary of a project
- The team or organizations doing the work
- The project's managers
- The project's sponsors, who finance the project
- Influential parties or organizations

Step 2: Map the List on the Grid

After generating the list of stakeholders, the group maps them into the matrix based on their relative power and interest. If the stakeholders have been captured on sticky notes, the group should be able to place them into the matrix directly.

Step 3: Develop a Strategy and Share It Broadly

After each stakeholder has been placed into the matrix, the group will want to discuss specific strategies for engaging their stakeholders. They may ask:

- Who needs to be informed of what, and when?

- Who needs to be consulted about what, and when?

- Who is responsible for engaging each stakeholder, and when and how will they do it?

Creating this draft is a good first step. If the project scope or number of stakeholders is large, it is advisable to share the analysis broadly and transparently with everyone involved. This validates the analysis by filling any gaps, and in the process, it clarifies where people fit in.

STRATEGY

Along with a RACI matrix and other "people + project" activities, stakeholder analysis is a basic framing tool for any project. For leaders and managers, it clearly scopes out who has what level of input and interest in a project, and can help to align decisions appropriately.

Although it has a long history, the source for the Stakeholder Analysis game is unknown.

Spectrum Mapping

OBJECT OF PLAY

Spectrum mapping is designed to reveal the diversity of perspectives and options around any given topic and to organize them into a meaningful spectrum. This game gives players an opportunity to express their views without having to assert them vocally or even take ownership of them in front of the group. It's valuable because it unearths information that plays a role in attitudes and behaviors that otherwise may not be visible.

NUMBER OF PLAYERS

5–15

DURATION OF PLAY

30 minutes to 1 hour

HOW TO PLAY

1. Before the game begins, brainstorm topics around which you want insight from the group. Write each topic on a sticky note.

2. Introduce Spectrum Mapping by stating that the purpose of the game is to illuminate the team's range of perspectives and to organize those perspectives into a continuum so that everyone gets a view of it.

3. Post the topic sticky notes in a column in the approximate middle of a space on the wall visible to the players. Ask everyone to silently generate a point-of-view preference option around that topic and write it on a sticky note. They are welcome to offer more than one.

4. Ask the players to come to the wall and post their sticky notes in a horizontal line on either side of the topic. Reassure them that the relationships between the sticky notes aren't yet of interest. The visual may look like the following figure.

5. Once the sticky notes are posted, work with the group to sort them into a horizontal range of ideas. Sticky notes that express similar perspectives or options should go next to each other. Sticky notes that seem to be outliers should stand alone; they may sometimes end up defining the limits of the range.

6. Continue sorting until the group agrees that the sticky notes are in their appropriate places on the horizontal line.

7. Repeat this process if you have more topics to evaluate.

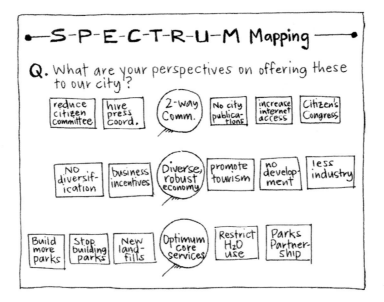

Once the spectrum for each topic has been laid along the horizon, ask for observations and insights on the lay of the land. Discuss the findings with the group and ask if any perspective or option has been excluded. If so, add it and re-sort as necessary.

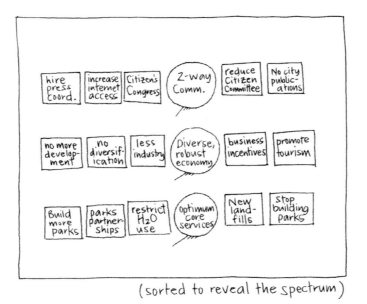

(sorted to reveal the spectrum)

STRATEGY

Not only does spectrum mapping reveal individual ideas around important topics, but it also tells you *how many* members of your group have certain types of views and where their endpoints lie. After spectrum mapping, the players are likely to discern a more holistic view of where they stand. In other words, spectrum mapping indicates whether the group tends to lean a certain way—perhaps it's fiscally conservative, oriented toward growth, or reticent about change. Either way, as a team leader, it's good to be aware of the group's natural inclination and openly acknowledge it to enhance future team building, problem solving, and planning.

Assure the players that they're free to write up honest perspectives and preferences around a topic even if those preferences may be considered outlandish by the other players. Tell them that outlier ideas still make it onto the continuum. This play is about mapping and displaying the spectrum, not evaluating ideas for validity, innovation, or popularity. This game has the effect of letting groups see if their behavior skews too far to one side or whether they're taking a reasonable approach when a radical one may be better.

The source for the Spectrum Mapping game is unknown.

Trading Cards

OBJECT OF PLAY

People sometimes grumble about the dreaded "icebreaker," but humans are like cars: we perform better when we're warmed up. This meeting starter is great because (1) it lets people self-define, (2) it gives people a "personality" outside the typical work environment, (3) it gives participants quick snapshots of multiple players (since they see many cards as they're being passed around), and (4) it creates memorable visuals that give people conversation pieces as the meeting progresses.

NUMBER OF PLAYERS

Unlimited

DURATION OF PLAY

10–15 minutes

HOW TO PLAY

1. Give the meeting participants access to large-scale index cards and markers.

2. Ask them to take 5–10 minutes to create a personal "trading card"—one that includes a self-portrait, a nickname for their "player," and one thing about themselves that people in the meeting aren't likely to know.

3. Have the players pass the trading cards around the room in no particular manner or order. Tell them to read each trading card that falls into their hands and hold onto one they might ask a question about. They can keep passing until they find one.

4. Ask for volunteers to read their player's name and nickname and then to ask that person a question related to the little-known fact on his card.

5. Let the player who was chosen elaborate on the question he was asked. The player can then opt to ask the person whose card he's holding a question, or he can pass and you can request another volunteer.

6. Keeping going around until the players appear to be sufficiently warmed up. But try to keep the play at or less than 15 minutes long.

STRATEGY

So, during the Trading Cards game, there really is no harm and, ahem, no foul. Help meeting participants integrate before the meeting starts.

The source of the Trading Cards game is unknown.

Visual Agenda

OBJECT OF PLAY

In a typical meeting, people walk in and are handed a typed sheet of paper that shows them the meeting agenda. It usually includes the date, the meeting topics, and the time allotted for each topic. Sometimes it acknowledges who is presenting or leading the topic. Most participants give this piece of paper about two seconds of their time. The standard approach for making agendas is perfectly fine for quick meetings among people who work together regularly. But for meetings that matter, for meetings that take a good amount of people's time and attention, and for meetings that bring together people from across disciplines or departments, visual agendas work much better.

When you create a visual agenda, people look it over and linger on it longer. They actually read the desired outcomes and review the steps they'll take to get there. The energy level rises when participants walk into a room and see a large, colorful, hand-drawn display. People start to talk about it with each other. A visual agenda implies that the day might be interesting; it sends a signal to the group that the meeting matters. Visuals also help participants recall later what the meeting was about.

HOW TO PLAY

1. Establish a desired outcome(s) for the meeting and craft an agenda that will get the group there. Choose a visual framework that represents the tone or theme of the meeting.

2. Draw the agenda in a nontraditional and creative way on a large sheet of paper or display it using presentation software.

STRATEGY

A visual agenda is a gesture to the group that you spent time before you took up theirs. So, take the time to build a good road map to your outcomes. And when drawing or creating the visual agenda, think of metaphors that represent a theme of the meeting. Draw pictures that symbolize the company's mission or work. If you're working at a vacation rental company, draw a beach scene with each footstep as a stage of the agenda. Draw a forest scene if you're working at an environmental organization; a circuit board if you're with a tech firm.

Brand the agenda in creative ways. If you've got copywriting chops, think of interesting phrases to describe each stage of the meeting. And if you have neither copywriter nor artistic instincts, ask someone who plans to attend the meeting to help you. Creating a visual agenda is a small investment in a meeting, but it offers a good ROI.

The Visual Agenda game was inspired by The Grove's practice of creating visual agendas before meetings.

Welcome to My World

OBJECT OF PLAY

Many of us make the mistaken assumption that others see what we see and know what we know. No one in the world shares your internal system map of reality. The best way to compare notes, so to speak, is to actually draw an external representation of what you think is happening. Welcome to My World gives players an opportunity to better understand other players' roles and responsibilities. It helps chip away at silos and introduces the novel idea that we may be seeing only one reality: ours. It helps immensely to show what we see to others so that we can start to share a reality and work on it together.

NUMBER OF PLAYERS

8–20

DURATION OF PLAY

30 minutes to 1 hour

HOW TO PLAY

1. Give all players access to flip-chart paper, markers, and sticky notes. Ask them to take 30 seconds to write one of their job responsibilities (e.g., create the company newsletter or devise a marketing strategy for Product X) on a sticky note and stick it to their shirt.

2. Have the players wander around the room and pair up with someone whose job responsibility they're the least familiar with or that they're curious about. If you have an odd number of players, join them to even it out.

3. In pairs, ask the players to take turns drawing their best representation of how they envision the other person's workflow around that job duty. They can use simple circles, boxes, and arrows to make flowcharts or they can get creative, but they cannot interview the other player or ask any clarifying questions while they're drawing. Give them 5–15 minutes to draw quietly.

4. When the time is up, give each player five minutes to share her drawing with the other person and describe what it means.

5. Then give the pairs 5–10 minutes each to clarify or agree on the realities of each other's drawing. They should also take time to discuss where the areas of ease, friction, and interactions with others fall in the process. They can elaborate and draw on the other person's visual at this point, or the original creator of the visual can add content as his partner shares.

6. Ask for volunteers to show their visuals to the larger group and to describe some of their insights and observations.

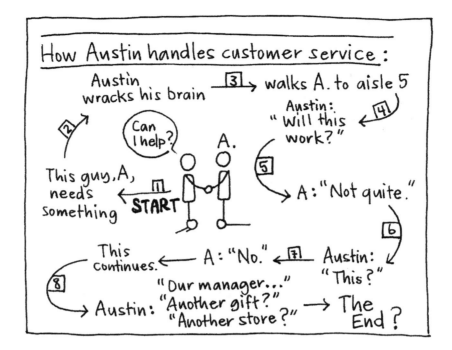

STRATEGY

To be maximally effective, this game has one requirement: the players should represent a range of positions or job responsibilities within an organization. The game rapidly loses its value if all the participants have the same, predictable workflow, like processing an undisputed insurance claim. The idea is to *educate* each other on the realities of their work duties and to help break down silos across organizational areas. Once the insights start coming out, this game can significantly increase the understanding and appreciation of others' work. And it can be even more effective when you have players who have to work together but historically have had little insight into—or even patience with—their colleagues' processes.

Most people feel comfortable drawing basic shapes and workflow-related diagrams since these are common in company life. If, however, players balk at having to draw, tell them they're welcome to rely only on words, but they'll miss an opportunity to make a simple picture of someone else's "world" at work.

The Welcome to My World game is credited to Sunni Brown.

CHAPTER 6

Games for Exploring

RARELY DO WE FIND EXACTLY WHAT WE WERE LOOKING FOR. The end result often emerges in surprising ways. Games that explore are for navigating, combining, interpreting, and otherwise working with ideas to discover something new.

Exploring games make and break patterns. In some cases they ask participants to create forms, and in others they ask them to split them apart. In most cases, exploring games are best used "in the middle" of an activity—before deciding and committing to action, but after the space has been framed and opened.

If we only opened raw ideas and then closed in on our favorites, we wouldn't create anything new. Games that explore chart the space in between.

The 4Cs

OBJECT OF PLAY
Simple information-splicing games come in handy because, in an intentional way, they disrupt the standard ways we break down topics. The 4Cs game is a quick way to gather and organize information about any subject using four common key concepts.

NUMBER OF PLAYERS
5–20

DURATION OF PLAY
30 minutes to 1 hour

HOW TO PLAY
1. Before the meeting, decide on a topic you want the players to explore and draw a 2×2 matrix in a large white space in the meeting room.

2. Write the following categories in each box of the matrix: "Components", "Characteristics", "Characters", and "Challenges". Then, draw something that represents each category.

3. Tell the players that this game is about exploring and sharing what they know about the topic based on the 4Cs. Define the terms of each "C":

   - **Components** are parts of the topic. For example, a component of a social commerce strategy might be responsive tweets. Components of a distribution channel might be 18-wheelers.

   - **Characteristics** are features of the topic. For example, speed of response is a characteristic of a social commerce strategy. A characteristic of an 18-wheeler might be an inefficient use of fuel.

   - **Challenges** are obstacles associated with the topic.

   - **Characters** are people associated with the topic.

You don't have to use four "Cs" to conduct this game. You can be creative with other letters that are company or team-specific. Use four "Ds" to create your matrix and name them "Discover", "Design", "Damage", and "Deliver". Just make sure the categories you create will give you a meaningful way to look at a topic of interest.

---

4. Divide the group into four teams of roughly equal size. (A group of 5–7 people can work as one team.) Give them access to sticky notes and markers.

5. Assign a different "C" to each team and tell them their goal is to collect information about that "C", specific to the topic. Tell them they'll have three minutes to plan an information-gathering strategy, five minutes to collect the information, and three minutes to analyze and organize it. Also explain that they should collect information from as many people in the room as possible.

6. Announce the start of the planning period, and let the teams converse with one another. At the end of three minutes, call time.

7. Tell the players they can use their sticky notes and markers, then kick off the five-minute information-gathering stage and stay out of the way. This stage of the game involves a lot of interviewing and moving around the room. Tell the players when the five minutes are up.

8. Start the three-minute information-analysis stage. In this stage, the players should analyze their data, organize it in a meaningful way, and post the contents in the matrix on the wall.

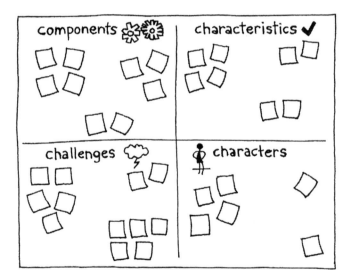

9. Close the game by asking for volunteers to present their group's findings. After each group presents, ask clarifying questions (Is there anything missing? Do these items mean the same thing?), and encourage the others to reflect on and add more information. You can also ask players if they want to share thoughts on their team's information-gathering process—to discuss what worked and what could have worked better.

STRATEGY

The 4Cs is deliberately quick (and slightly chaotic) to avoid a situation in which people simply list information about what they know related to the topic. In this game, the players gathering information may already have a lot of detail about the topic, but they'll inevitably learn something new through the process of interviewing others. Interviewing allows people who may not interact much the opportunity to do so. Because the time is short, they won't dive into a substantive conversation; nevertheless, the chances are higher that someone will take away new content or a new perspective based on an interview.

Avoid shortchanging the closing activity, even though it may be tempting to give the group more time to gather and analyze their content (and some of them will request it). The last stage of the game is important to spend time on because it allows the group to reflect on the content together, as a sort of group mind. If the meeting is based on a familiar topic, there will likely be many players who think they have a corner on information around it, so it's important to discuss the 4Cs as a whole group. It exposes more ground to more people and invites a discussion that can bring new life to old content.

The 4Cs is based on the same-named activity written by Matthew Richter in the March 2004 publication of the Thiagi GameLetter.

The 5 Whys

OBJECT OF PLAY

Many of the games in this book are about seeing the bigger picture or relating a problem to its context. The 5 Whys game mirrors that motive to move beyond the surface of a problem and discover the root cause, because problems are tackled more sustainably when they're addressed at the source.

NUMBER OF PLAYERS

5–10

HOW TO PLAY

1. Prior to the meeting, establish a problem your team needs to evaluate. Write the problem in an area visible to all the group members, and if you'd like, draw something that represents it.

2. Distribute sticky notes to each player and ask them to number five of them 1 through 5.

3. Ask the players to review the problem statement and ask themselves WHY it's a problem. Then ask them to write their first response on sticky note 1.

4. Tell the players to ask themselves WHY the answer on sticky note 1 is true and write their next response on sticky note 2.

5. Again, tell the players to ask themselves WHY the answer on sticky note 2 is true and write the response on sticky note 3.

6. Repeat this process in numerical order until every numbered sticky note has a response written on it.

7. Below the problem statement, write the word "Why?" five times in a column and draw lines to create columns for each player's set of notes. Ask the players to approach the wall and post their responses, starting with 1 at the top and ending with 5 on the bottom.

8. Review the "Why" columns with the group and note commonalities and differences. Allow for discussion.

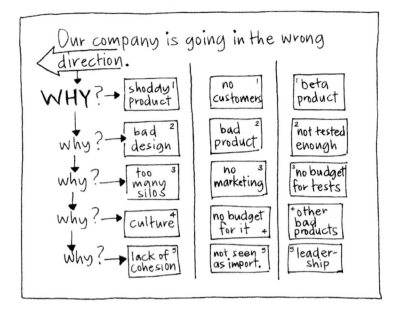

Rewrite the problem statement on a sheet of flip-chart paper. Then give a volunteer five clean sticky notes to write on, and work with the group to build consensus on which of the five "Whys" in the columns offer the most meaningful insight into the problem. Ask the volunteer to rewrite the "Whys"—one per sticky note—as the group agrees on them. Once they're all written, tape the five index cards into a final column under the problem statement. If you have time, move into a discussion around "what's next."

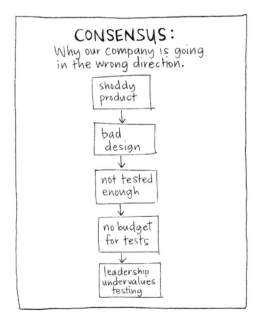

STRATEGY

This game is about reading more between the lines—about understanding the root cause of a problem so that people can get the greatest leverage out of solving it. When leading this game, encourage the players to be honest. This is the single most important strategy. If the players avoid the issues, the game doesn't yield good information. And in a worst-case scenario, you could have people actually addressing the wrong problems. So, as the meeting leader, be aware of the dynamics between the players and foster open conversation around the difficult question of "why".

Another important practice is to ask the players to write the first thing that comes to mind each time they ask "Why?". If they jump immediately to the perceived root of the problem, they may miss the opportunity to see the stages, which are valuable to know for problem solving at different levels.

Finally, many problems require more or less interrogation to get to the root. Ask "Why?" until you feel the group is really getting somewhere. Five Whys is a healthy place to start, but don't interpret it as a fixed number. Build longer WHY columns if necessary, and keep going until you get the players to meaningful insights.

The 5 Whys game is based on a game by Sakichi Toyoda.

Affinity Map

OBJECT OF PLAY

Most of us are familiar with brainstorming—a method by which a group generates as many ideas around a topic as possible in a limited amount of time. Brainstorming works to get a high quantity of information on the table. But it prompts the follow-up question of how to gather meaning from all the data. Using a simple Affinity Diagram technique can help us discover embedded patterns (and sometimes break old patterns) of thinking by sorting and clustering language-based information into relationships. It can also give us a sense of where most people's thinking is focused. Use an affinity diagram when you want to find categories and meta-categories within a cluster of ideas and when you want to see which ideas are most common within the group.

NUMBER OF PLAYERS

Up to 20

DURATION OF PLAY

Depends on the number of players, but a maximum of 1.5 hours

HOW TO PLAY

1. On a sheet of flip-chart paper, write a question the players will respond to along with a visual that complements it. Conduct this game only when you have a question for the players that you know will generate at least 20 pieces of information to sort.

2. Ask each player to take 10 minutes to generate sticky notes in response to the question. Use index cards on a table if you have a group of four or less. Conduct this part of the process silently.

3. Collect the ideas from the group and post them on a flat working surface visible to everyone. It should end up resembling the following figure.

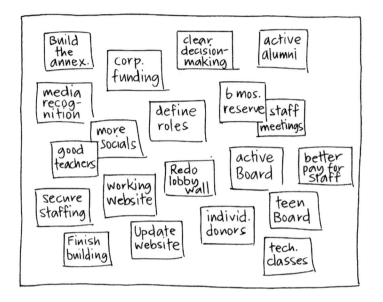

4. Based on guidance from the players, sort the ideas into columns (or clusters) based on relationships. Involve the group in the process as much as possible. Have the players approach the wall to post their notes—it saves time—and allow them to do an initial, general sorting in columns or clusters.

5. Create a sticky-note "parking lot" close to the display for ideas that don't appear to fall into a natural category. Redundancy in ideas is OK; don't discard sticky notes because they're already represented. It's helpful to leave repeated ideas posted since it indicates to the group how many people are thinking the same thing. At this stage, ask the players to try to avoid searching for higher categories and simply to focus on grouping the information based on the affinities.

6. Once the content is sorted, ask the group to suggest categories that represent the columns you've created and write the categories they agree on at the top of the column (or near a cluster if you chose a cluster rather than a column display). Don't let the players spend an inordinate amount of time agreeing on a name for a category. If there's disagreement over "Facilities" versus "Infrastructure," write them both. If the players produce categories that are significantly different, pay attention to which category gets the most approval from the group and write that one. Your visual may end up looking like the following.

STRATEGY

The value of the Affinity Diagram game increases when two conditions are met. The first is that the players generate multiple data points, ideally with good information. The second relates to the quality of the sorting. The cleaner the players' insights when they form relationships within the content, the better the categories will be.

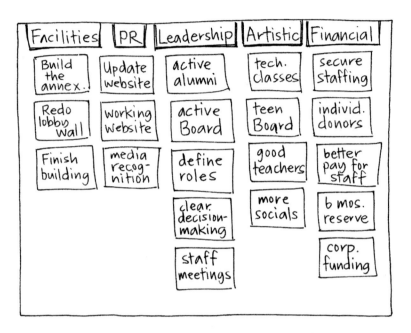

Sometimes affinities within content are crystal clear, so the sorting becomes less pivotal, but when those relationships are more nuanced, it's more important that the sorting process is done well. In a situation in which there are many ways to affinitize information, assume a stronger facilitative role. Ask questions about the columns or clusters to clarify the group's thinking and steer them toward an appropriate number of categories. If there are too many, the data gets watered down. If there are too few, the analysis gets watered down. Help the players find the sweet spot.

Optional activity: Run through the Affinity Diagram game once, complete with categorizations. Then ask the group to reshuffle the sticky notes and recombine the ideas based on affinities they didn't notice in the first round.

The affinity diagram was devised by Jiro Kawakita in the 1960s. It is also referred to as the KJ Method.

Atomize

OBJECT OF PLAY

There is a time to go deep. Just as in science, breaking large structures into their base components is fundamental to knowledge work. It is how we create understanding and formulate new ideas.

This exercise starts with a single item and ends with a layer-by-layer analysis of its components. It is useful for unpacking large but poorly understood structures. Although the applications are numerous, some structures that are well suited for atomization include:

- A firm's offering
- A technology platform
- An enterprise-wide initiative
- A supply or demand chain
- A group's culture or other "intangible"

By breaking the larger system into its components, the group will have an advantage in problem solving or brainstorming. Because they are more discreet and tangible, the smaller components are more easily handled and better understood. Likewise, the overall map that is created will help serve as an explanation of the overall system.

NUMBER OF PLAYERS

Small groups

DURATION OF PLAY

1 hour or more

HOW TO PLAY

1. Open the exercise by putting the name of the system on a sticky note at the top of a large whiteboard. Introduce the exercise as a way to understand what the system is made of in tangible terms, by breaking it down into its "atoms."

2. To start the brainstorming, ask the group to "split" the main system into its components. In this step you are generating a list of things to capture on sticky notes directly below the main topic. Generally, a short list of three to five large components is the norm.

3. For each item, repeat the splitting process by asking "What combines to create this?" In this manner, you will build a pyramid of components all the way down.

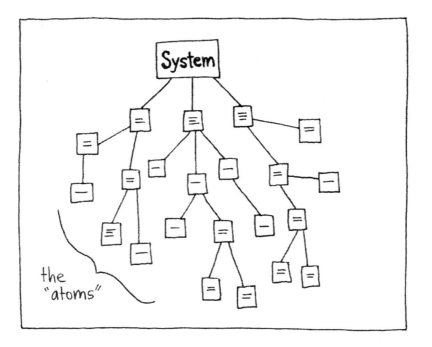

The map and individual components that result may be used as inputs into other activities, or may be documented as an explanation of a system's parts.

STRATEGY

At some point, usually four to five levels deep, there is a natural turning point. Instead of becoming more diverse, the items start to become more fundamental. This is the atomic level, and where some of the most interesting results are found. In exploring a group's culture, this is where hidden attitudes and behaviors unique to the group may be discovered. In atomizing a service offering or product, this is where elementary characteristics and differentiation points may live.

The Atomize game is credited to James Macanufo.

The Blind Side

OBJECT OF PLAY

Every human being has blind spots and every company does, too. Knowledge openness can enhance businesses and relationships while knowledge blindness can make things unnecessarily more difficult. In other words, what we don't know can hurt us. The military refers to this as "the fog of war." The premise of this game, therefore, is to disclose and discover unknown information that can impact organizational and group success in any area of the company—management, planning, team performance, and so forth.

NUMBER OF PLAYERS

5–15

DURATION OF PLAY

30–45 minutes

HOW TO PLAY

1. Before the meeting, decide on a topic for discussion. Draw a large-scale profile of a person and draw four arrows coming out of the top of the head. Label those arrows "Know/Know", "Know/Don't Know", "Don't Know/Know", and "Don't Know/Don't Know".

2. Give the players access to sticky notes and markers and tell them that the purpose of this game is to try to make explicit the knowledge they have, and the knowledge they don't have but could use.

3. Start with the Know/Know category. Elicit from the group all information about the topic that they know they know. This category should go quickly and should generate a lot of content. Ask the players to write one bit of knowledge per sticky note and cluster them near the arrow pertaining to that category. (They'll do this for each category.)

4. Next, tackle Know/Don't Know. This category will go less quickly than the first but should still generate plenty of content. Again, ask them to cluster the sticky notes near the related arrow.

5. Move to Don't Know/Know. This information could be skills people have that are currently not used to solve problems or untapped resources that have been forgotten.

6. Last, move to Don't Know/Don't Know. The group will be stopped here, possibly indefinitely. This category is where discovery and shared exploration take place. Ask the players provocative questions: What does this team know that your team doesn't know it doesn't know? How can you find out what you don't know you don't know?

7. Ask the group what they can do to proactively address the distinct challenges of each category. Discuss insights and "aha's". Even if the players' only revelation is that they have blind spots, this in itself can be a fruitful discovery.

STRATEGY

This game works best with a familiar team when the participants cross disciplines and responsibilities. Having a diverse group enhances the feedback loop for the Don't Know categories, which are where the players are going to get stuck. They'll be confident about what they know—and even about what they know they don't know—but without an outside perspective, it's next to impossible to declare what we don't know we don't know. The nature of this question warrants discussion and the solicitation of others' observations.

Because this game has an obvious trust-building component, start by sharing easy information and move toward more substantive information depending on the players' comfort level. Keep the group on business- or project-related topics and away from personal evaluations. Although The Blind Side can be used as a psychological assessment, the self-help applications of this game should be conducted outside the business setting, unless you're dealing with the rare group that's into that.

The Blind Side is inspired by and adapted from the Johari Window, a communication model developed by Joseph Luft and Harry Ingham. The game variation of the model is credited to Sunni Brown.

Build the Checklist

OBJECT OF PLAY

In all work of reasonable complexity, there is a moment-to-moment risk that equally important tasks will overwhelm the human mind. In knowledge work this may be doubly true, due to the intangible "fuzziness" of any particular task. For groups that are charting out how they will work one of the most practical and useful things they can do is build a checklist.

Although creating a checklist may seem like an open-and-shut exercise, often it uncovers a manifest of issues. Because a checklist is a focusing object, it demands that the team discuss the order and importance of certain tasks. Team members are likely to have different perspectives on these things, and the checklist is a means to bring these issues to the surface and work with them.

NUMBER OF PLAYERS

A small team that has deep experience with the task at hand

DURATION OF PLAY

1 hour or more, depending on the task to be analyzed

HOW TO PLAY

It's most useful to create the checklist in order of operation, from first to last, but in some cases a ranked or prioritized list is more appropriate. Consider which the group would benefit more from creating.

1. To begin, introduce to the group the topic at hand: "You will be creating a checklist for doing [fill in the blank]." It may be useful to prime the group into thinking about a particular situation or duration of time, as in "Getting from A to B" or "Dealing with an Angry Customer."

2. Have the group brainstorm tasks to put on the checklist using sticky notes. Guide the group to create items that are concrete and measurable, like a switch that is turned on or off. For example, "assess arrival readiness" is not as useful as "deploy landing gear."

3. Once the group has generated a pool of ideas, they may use Post-Up and affinity mapping to remove duplicate tasks. In discussing what has been added to the list, two things may be done:

- Have the group order the tasks into a procedure. Use sticky notes so that the individual tasks can be moved. Given a space with a beginning and an end, the group can discuss and debate the ordering while creating the list in real time.

- Have the group force-rank the tasks. In this case, the group must decide the order of importance of the tasks. By doing this, the group may be able to agree to cut items from the bottom of the list, making their checklist shorter and more direct.

In all cases, the discussion and reflection that come out of the initial brainstorming will be where the most progress is made. It is likely that new ideas will surface and be added to the checklist in the discussion. Coming out of the discussion the group's next step is to capture the checklist as an artifact and share it with others who can test it and improve it.

The Build the Checklist game is credited to James Macanufo.

Business Model Canvas

OBJECT OF PLAY

New business models can rapidly disrupt an entire industry—just look what Apple's iTunes strategy did to the music industry. The Business Model Canvas, developed by Alex Osterwalder, is a tool that you can use to examine and rethink a business model.

NUMBER OF PLAYERS

1–6. Works well individually to quickly sketch out and think through an idea. To map an organization's existing or future business model you should work in groups. The more diverse the group of players, the more accurate the picture of the business model will be.

DURATION OF PLAY

Anywhere between 15 minutes for individual play, 2-4 hours to map an organization's existing business model, and up to two days to develop a future or start-up business model.

HOW TO PLAY

Mapping business models works best when players work on a poster on the wall. Print a large scale version of the canvas or create one by drawing out the categories on the wall. The canvas is downloadable at *businessmodelhub.com*. If drawing it out, a version might look like this:

Make sure all players have access to markers and sticky notes of varying sizes and colors. You will also need a camera to capture the results.

There are several games and variations you can play with the Business Model Canvas Poster. Here we describe the most basic game, which is the mapping of an organization's existing business model, its assessment, and the formulation of improved or potential new business models. This can easily be adapted to the objectives of the players.

1. A good way to start mapping your business model is by letting players begin to describe the different customer segments your organization serves. Players should put up different color sticky notes on the canvas poster for each type of segment. A group of customers represents a distinct segment if they have distinct needs and you offer them distinct value propositions (e.g. a newspapers serves readers and advertisers), or if they require different channels, customer relationships, or revenue streams.

2. Subsequently, players should map out the value propositions your organization offers each customer segment. Players should use same color sticky notes for value propositions and customer segments that go together. If a value proposition targets two very different customer segments, the sticky note colors of both segments should be used.

3. Then players should map out all the remaining building blocks of your organization's business model with sticky notes. They should always try to use the colors of the related customer segment.

4. When the players mapped out the whole business model they can start assessing its strength and weaknesses by putting up green (strength) and red (weakness) sticky notes alongside the strong and weak elements of the mapped business model. Alternatively, sticky notes marked with a "+" and "-" can be used rather than colors.

5. Based on the visualization of your organization's business model, which players mapped out in steps 1-4, they can now either try to improve the existing business model or generate totally new alternative business models. Ideally players use one or several additional Business Model Canvas Posters to map out improved business models or new alternatives.

STRATEGY

The mapping of an organization's existing business model, including its strengths and weaknesses, is an essential starting point to improve the current business model and/ or develop new future business models. At the very least the game leads to a refined and shared understanding of an organization's business model. At its best it helps players develop strategic directions for the future by outlining new and/or improved business models for the organization.

The Business Model Canvas was designed by Alexander Osterwalder and Yves Pigneur. The poster is available under the Creative Commons license as a free download at http://www. businessmodelhub.com. *It is also featured in their book,* Business Model Generation.

Button

OBJECT OF PLAY

A common element of brainstorming or group work is the "let's go around and hear from everyone" routine. The rule governing this is a valuable one—that everyone speaks once before anyone speaks twice.

There are two problems with this, however. First, moving from one person to the next in a round-robin fashion can be an energy drain, even with a small number of people. It's predictable, and the participants at the end of the line are often short-changed. Second, and potentially more damaging to the activity, is that often a participant's attention wanes when she is "on deck" and preparing her own thoughts as opposed to listening to others.

The Button is a simple technique that keeps true to the original rule while avoiding the traps of a round robin.

HOW TO PLAY

When the group is asked to report on a question, a small token—it may be a poker chip or something similar—is given to the first volunteer to respond. After his response, he chooses a person who has yet to speak to take the button. This continues until everyone has spoken once.

> *This can be done easily with index cards instead of a button. Participants think about their answers to a question first and write a word on the card along with their name. The cards are passed to the left in a quick manner for a few moments so that in the process of passing the order becomes scrambled. The participants then call on each other by way of reading the words aloud and asking the writers to explain.*

STRATEGY

Randomization keeps the participants' attention. When you don't know if you will be called on next, you will be more present and focused. The Button game also passes control onto the participants, by giving them the power to nominate the next speaker.

The Button is inspired by the Native American "Talking Stick" tradition, where a ceremonial object such as a stick or feather, representing the right to speak, was passed from one person to another to respect speakers and avoid interruptions.

Campfire

OBJECT OF PLAY

Employees spend hours sitting in training sessions, sifting through orientation manuals, and playing corporate e-learning games to learn the know-how for their new positions. But the reality is that the bulk of employee knowledge is gained through storytelling. Employees train each other by sharing their personal and professional experiences. Campfire leverages our natural storytelling tendencies by giving players a format and a space in which to share work stories—of trial and error, failure and success, competition, diplomacy, and teamwork. Campfire is useful not only because it acts as an informal training game, but also because it reveals commonalities in employee perception and experience.

NUMBER OF PLAYERS

8–20

DURATION OF PLAY

30–45 minutes

HOW TO PLAY

1. Before the meeting, brainstorm 10–20 words or phrases you can use as trigger words to start the storytelling session. Write them on sticky notes. Keep the ideas positive or neutral: partnership, venture, first day, work travel, fun project, opportunity, and so forth.

2. Post the sticky notes in the meeting room in a space visible to all the players and give them access to markers and more sticky notes. Tell them that this is a workplace "campfire" and the only thing they're invited to do is share stories back and forth as an informal "company training program." Show them the "wall of words" and ask them to take 1–3 minutes to look them over and recall a story associated with one of them. To help the group warm up, start the storytelling session yourself by removing one of the words on the wall and posting it in a space nearby. Then tell your introductory story.

3. Ask for a volunteer to continue what you started by peeling another word from the wall and posting it next to yours. This begins the sticky-note "story thread."

4. Before the first player begins his story, ask him to read aloud the word he chose and then instruct the other players to listen carefully to his story and to jot down a word or phrase on a sticky note that reminds them of another work-related story. If no words in the player's story jumped out at them, they are welcome to pull a sticky note from your original "wall of words."

5. After the player concludes the first story, ask for another volunteer to approach the wall and to either post her own sticky note or take one from the "wall of words." Ask her to read her word aloud and to then share her story.

6. Repeat this process until the players have created a snake-like "story thread" which acts as an archive of the campfire conversation. Use your best judgment to determine when to end the storytelling session. Before you "put out" the fire, ask the players if there are any lessons learned or final thoughts they want to add.

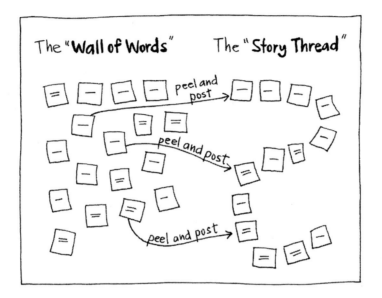

STRATEGY

Your role as the meeting leader is simply to encourage the sharing of work-related stories. If you find a lull in the storytelling thread, refer the employees back to the "wall of words" or ask someone to throw out a "wildcard" story. You can also share work-related stories of your own that are triggered by stories from the players. You can let the stories drift toward less positive or neutral topics if you think the players need some catharsis, but be prepared to manage what may come up and don't let the meeting conclude on a sour note.

The point of Campfire is simple but powerful. It encourages sharing, shows the many things employees have in common, and leverages the natural tendency of employee training to take place through informal dialogue. Humans want to tell stories; you'll likely find that the players linger to share experiences even after the meeting ends.

This game was inspired by Tell Me a Story: Narrative and Intelligence (Rethinking Theory), by Roger Schank and Gary Saul Morson and is credited to Sunni Brown.

Challenge Cards

OBJECT OF PLAY

To identify and think through challenges, problems and potential pitfalls in a product, service or strategy.

NUMBER OF PLAYERS

Works best with small groups of 5-10

HOW TO PLAY

Divide each group into two teams. One team, the "solution team" silently brainstorms features and strengths of the product or solution. The other team, the "challenge team" silently brainstorms potential problems or challenges and writes them on index cards, one problem or challenge per card.

When play commences, the two teams work together to tell a collaborative story. The challenge team picks a card from the deck and plays it on the table, describing a scene or event where the issue might realistically arise. The solution team must then pick a card from their deck that addresses the challenge. If they have a solution they get a point, and if they don't have a solution the challenge team gets a point. The teams then work together to design a card that addresses that challenge. Play continues in this fashion, challenge followed by solution followed by challenge, and so on, until the story or scenario reaches a conclusion.

STRATEGY

The goal of this game is to improve a product or strategy by thinking through various scenarios and alternatives. By turning the exercise into a competition as well as a storytelling game, players are more likely to get engaged and immerse themselves in the scenarios. Keeping it lighthearted and fun will increase the energy. It shouldn't feel like work.

This game emerged spontaneously during a Gamestorming workshop in London in 2010.

Customer, Employee, Shareholder

OBJECT OF PLAY
The object of this game is to imagine possible futures from multiple perspectives.

NUMBER OF PLAYERS
1–10

DURATION OF PLAY
1–3 hours

HOW TO PLAY

1. Divide your group into three roles: Customers, Employees, and Shareholders.

2. Ask the players to step into their roles and imagine their business five years from now. What will they value? What will their experience be like? What events or trends emerge? What specific, tangible things are different?

3. Have the players draw their visions of the future and share them.

4. Ask the group to identify themes and new possibilities. Capture them and consult the group on next steps.

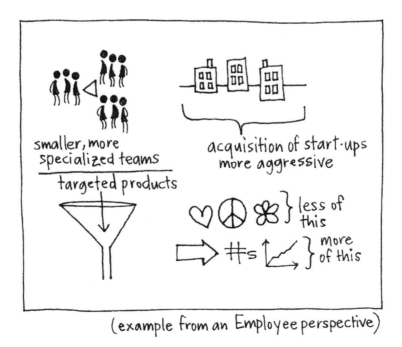

(example from an Employee perspective)

STRATEGY

In this exercise, the group is given a chance to relate intuitive knowledge about the business that may not surface otherwise. If possible, allow the group to cycle through multiple roles by reshuffling the roles and repeating the exercise.

The Customer, Employee, Shareholder game is based on the Stakeholder Framework developed by Max Clarkson in "A Stakeholder Framework for Analyzing and Evaluating Corporate Social Performance" in the Academy of Management Review (1995).

Design the Box

Before you begin, focus on the end. In this exercise, teams create the physical "box" that sells their idea—whether that idea will ultimately become a tangible product or not. By imagining the package for their idea, the teams make decisions about important features and other aspects of their vision that are more difficult to articulate.

This game is popular among software developers when setting out to capture the customer's view of a new application, but its use doesn't stop there. The game can help facilitate any vision-oriented discussion, and has been used to describe topics ranging from "our future methodology" to "the ideal hire."

In all cases, the box is a focusing device: it wraps up a lot of otherwise intangible information into a nice physical object, prompting decisions along the way. When teams present or "sell" their boxes to each other, a number of things come to life, including the natural translation of features into benefits. Also, it's fun to do. The results of the exercise may be simple drawings or an actual box, which may live on well after as a friendly reminder of the big picture.

NUMBER OF PLAYERS:

Although the exercise may be done with a small group, teams working in parallel on different boxes will result in a more robust discussion during the "selling phase."

DURATION OF PLAY:

1 hour or more, depending on the number of groups and depth of discussion.

SETUP

Although paper and markers will work for drawing a box, don't hesitate to bring heavier craft supplies to bear. Consider acquiring blank white cardboard boxes from an office supply or mailing store. Markers, craft paper, stickers, tape and scissors are all worth the investment.

It may help get the group's creative gears moving by having sample boxes handy. Cereal boxes, with their free prize offers, bold imagery and nutritional information, are good thought starters. Likewise, plain "store-label" boxes, gift boxes and toy boxes offer a range of voices. A group that is heavily entrenched in the business-as-usual paradigm will benefit the most from having this inspiration at hand.

HOW TO PLAY

The exercise moves through three phases: an introduction, box creation and sharing by "selling."

Phase One: Fill the Box

Before a group can jump into creating a box, they need to reflect on what could be in it. To get people oriented, consider laying out some building blocks:

- Possible names of the idea

- Possible customers, end users, or buyers

- Possible features, functions, or other important defining details

This may be familiar ground, or it may be entirely new to the group. They key in setting up the exercise is to give teams "just enough" information to feel comfortable starting.

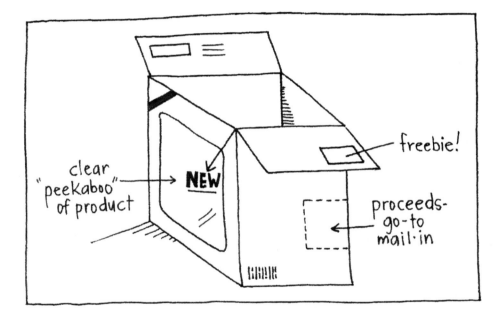

Phase Two: Make the Box

Give the teams a set amount of time, 30 minutes or more, to create the box for their idea. Ask them to imagine coming across the box on a retail shelf, shrink-wrapped and ready for sale. In designing the box, teams may be helped by a few of these prompts:

- What's it called?

- Who's it for?

- What's its tagline or slogan?

- What are its most compelling features? Benefits?

- What imagery would make it stand out to you?

Teams may self-organize naturally; most participants will want to create their own box regardless of how they're arranged. Make sure you have ample supplies for them to do so, and make sure they know that there is no wrong way to create their box.

Phase Three: Sell the Box

Each team or individual should be offered the chance to stand up and "sell" their boxes back to the group. It may be worthwhile to keep a timer for these stand-up presentations, and consider offering a prize to the team that does the best job "selling" their box back to the group.

Look for a naturally occurring breakthrough as they present back their boxes. People put features on the box, but when they sell them, they translate those features into benefits. Listen for the phrases "so that" or "because," which bridge otherwise mechanical features into living benefits.

The exercise works well as an open-ended, divergent process, but may be run so that the teams converge on an agreed-upon, shared box. If agreement and alignment is a desired outcome of the exercise, note the differences and similarities in how each team interpreted their box. Build on the common ground captured in the similarities, and isolate differences for discussion. Consider running a second round, this time incorporating these agreements into a final shared box.

In any case, if there is a prize to be awarded for the best "box seller," make sure it's the teams that cast the votes. And have enough prizes so that if the box was created by a team everyone on the team will have a prize.

STRATEGY

Keep the boxes and display them in a prominent place. These may be more valuable (and visible) artifacts than any other documentation that comes out of the exercise. It may also be beneficial to record the presentations the teams give around their boxes, if it is not disruptive to the flow of the group.

The core act of "designing the box" may be altered to work for different contexts and participants.

This exercise goes by many names, and there are a number of good sources to look to for its variations. This version is based on and adapted from the game Product Box in Luke Hohmann's book, Innovation Games: Creating Breakthrough Products Through Collaborative Play. *Other sources point to Jim Highsmith of the Cutter Consortium, and to Bill Shackelford of Shackelford & Associates with the origination of the concept.*

Do, Redo & Undo

When creating something, it's easier to think in the affirmative. We think in a vector of taking actions and building things, and can forget that over time undoing those same decisions can be just as important. Do, Redo & Undo asks a group to focus on this, and to think through the implications of dismantling and altering.

This is a useful exercise in developing any human-to-machine or human-to-human system. Software provides myriad cases of undoing: users need to change configurations, fix mistakes, and remove software entirely. Business processes need to address this equally well: components need to change or dissolve, and often this flexibility is lost without clarity on how it is done.

NUMBER OF PLAYERS

Small groups

DURATION OF PLAY

1 hour or more, depending on the complexity of the existing "Best-Case Scenario"

HOW TO PLAY

The Best-Case Scenario

Generally, the group would run this exercise after they have a concept or prototype as a starting point. In the case of software, it may be a user story or feature list; in a process, it may be a draft of the flow.

The group should be given time to walk through and digest this example. The exercise opens with the group brainstorming answers to a simple question: "What mistakes can and will be made?"

Using Post-Up, the group brainstorms a set of items on sticky notes and pools them to create a starting set of scenarios to explore "undoing and redoing." It's not unusual for a few humorous items to make the list. Other questions to consider asking in fleshing out the set include:

- "What would happen if a group of monkeys tried to use it?"

- "What happens if we pull the plug? Where is the plug?"

The Worst-Case Scenario

In generating the initial list in Post-Up, the group has identified at least one Worst-Case Scenario. Their task now is to address the items by focusing on three possible solutions:

Do: Change the design or plan to avoid the problem altogether. This takes the issue off the table.

Redo: Provide a means for altering action while it's being taken. This may be a course correction or a buffering of the situation's impact.

Undo: Provide a means for completely undoing an action and returning to a previously known state. This completely abandons the scenario.

A group that has a large number of items in the **Worst-Case Scenario** may wish to prioritize them by likelihood and then focus on the hotspots. There is an implied order of preference in Do, Redo & Undo. A problem that can be entirely eliminated by changing the design avoids needing a "redo" or "undo" solution. For example, a feature that asks the user to enter her contact information might be eliminated entirely, if the information can be fetched from somewhere else.

As the group works through Do, Redo & Undo, they should capture their solutions and revisit the original **Best-Case Scenario**. Their draft of solutions should accompany the design as it matures, eventually proving itself in user testing and the real world.

The Do, Redo & Undo game is credited to James Macanufo.

Elevator Pitch

OBJECT OF PLAY

What has been a time-proven exercise in product development applies equally well in developing any new idea: writing the elevator pitch. When developing and communicating a vision for something, whether it's a new service, a company-wide initiative, or just a good idea that merits spreading, a group will benefit from going through the exercise of writing their elevator pitch.

Often this is the hardest thing to do in developing a new idea. An elevator pitch must be short enough to deliver in a fictional elevator ride but also contain a compelling description of the problem you're solving, who you'll solve it for, and one key benefit that distinguishes it from other ideas.

NUMBER OF PLAYERS

Can be done individually, or with a small working group

DURATION OF PLAY

Save at least 90 minutes for the entire exercise, and consider a short break after the initial idea generation is complete before prioritizing and shaping the pitch itself. Small working groups will have an easier time coming to a final pitch; in some cases it may be necessary to assign one person with follow-up accountability for the final wording after the large decisions have been made in the exercise.

HOW TO PLAY

Going through the exercise involves both a generating and a formative phase. To set up the generating phase, write these headers in sequence on flip charts:

- Who is the target customer?
- What is the customer need?
- What is the product name?
- What is its market category?
- What is its key benefit?
- Who or what is the competition?
- What is the product's unique differentiator?

These will become the elements of the elevator pitch. They are in a sequence that adheres to the following formula.

```
Elevator Pitch sentence
structure:
FOR (target customer), WHO HAS
(customer need), (product name) IS A
(market category) THAT (one key benefit).
UNLIKE (competition), THE
PRODUCT (unique differentiator).
```

To finish the setup, explain the elements and their connection to each other.

The *target customer* and *customer need* are deceptively simple: any relatively good idea or product will likely have many potential customers and address a greater number of needs. In the generative phase, all of these are welcome ideas.

It is helpful to fix the *product name* in advance—this will help contain the scope of the conversation and focus the participants on "what" the pitch is about. It is not outside the realm of possibility, however, that useful ideas will be generated in the course of the exercise that relate to the product name, so it may be left open to interpretation.

The *market category* should be an easily understood description of the type of idea or product. It may sound like "employee portal" or "training program" or "peer-to-peer community." The category gives an important frame of reference for the target customer, from which they will base comparisons and perceive value.

The *key benefit* will be one of the hardest areas for the group to shape in the final pitch. This is the single most compelling reason a target customer would buy into the idea. In an elevator pitch, there is no time to confuse the matter with multiple benefits—there can be only one memorable reason "why to buy." However, in the generative phase, all ideas are welcome.

The *competition* and *unique differentiator* put the final punctuation on the pitch. Who or what will the target customer compare this idea to, and what's unique about this idea?

In some cases, the *competition* may literally be another firm or product. In other cases, it may be "the existing training program" or "the last time we tried a big change initiative." The *unique differentiator* should be just that: *unique* to this idea or approach, in a way that distinguishes it in comparison to the competition.

The Generating Phase

Once the elements are understood, participants brainstorm ideas on sticky notes that fit under each header. At first, they should generate freely, without discussion or analysis, any ideas that fit into any of the categories. Using the Post-Up technique, participants put their notes onto the flip charts and share their ideas.

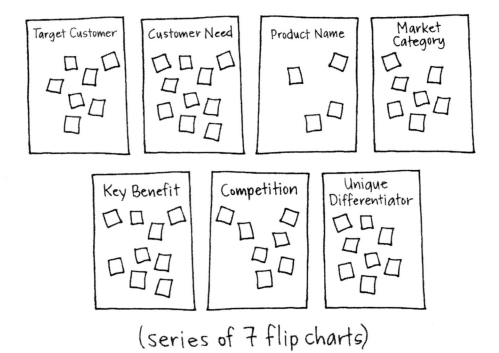

Next, the group may discuss areas where they have the most trouble on their current pitch. Do we know enough about the competition to claim a unique differentiator? Do we agree on a target customer? Is our market category defined, or are we trying to define something new? Where do we need to focus?

Before stepping into the formative phase, the group may use dot voting, affinity mapping, or another method to prioritize and cull their ideas in each category.

The Formative Phase

Following a discussion and reflection on the possible elements of a pitch, the group then has the task of "trying out" some possibilities.

This may be done by breaking into small groups, as pairs, or as individuals, depending on the size of the larger group. Each group is given the task of writing an elevator pitch, based on the ideas on the flip charts.

After a set amount of time (15 minutes may be sufficient), the groups reconvene and present their draft versions of the pitch. The group may choose to role-play as a target customer while listening to the pitch, and comment or ask questions of the presenters.

The exercise is complete when there is a strong direction among the group on what the pitch should *and should not* contain. One potential outcome is the crafting of distinct pitches for different target customers; you may direct the group to focus on this during the formative stage.

STRATEGY

Don't aim for final wording with a large group. It's an achievement if you can get to that level of completion, but it's not critical and can be shaped after the exercise. What is important is that the group decides what is and is not a part of the pitch.

Role play is the fastest way to test a pitch. Assuming the role of a customer (or getting some real customers to participate in the exercise) will help filter out the jargon and empty terms that may interfere with a clear pitch. If the pitch is truly believable and compelling, participants should have no problem making it real with customers.

The elevator pitch, or elevator speech, is a traditional staple of the venture capital community, based on the idea that if you are pitching a business idea it should be simple enough to convey on a short elevator ride.

Five-Fingered Consensus

OBJECT OF PLAY

Like Red/Green Cards (discussed later in this chapter), this is a technique for managing the feedback loop between a facilitator and a large group. When working in breakouts or as a large group, it may be necessary to periodically gauge the level of perceived consensus, without spending an unnecessary amount of time talking about it. A facilitator may ask for this quickly by using the "five-fingers check."

HOW TO PLAY

The facilitator asks the group to rate their level of consensus on a topic from 0 to 5, with five fingers meaning "absolute, total agreement" and a fist meaning "completely different points of view." This is particularly useful in managing breakout groups, where different topics may be discussed simultaneously. A group that holds up a variety of ones, twos, and threes may have more work to do.

STRATEGY

The "trick" in this technique is in gauging how far apart the individuals feel they are from consensus. A group that is wide apart in the view of its members—with some holding up five fingers and others holding up two—may need outside support and mediation of their discussion.

Hand signals are a commonly found element of consensus-based decision making and dispute resolution. Related is the thumbs-up, thumbs-down, and thumbs-sideways technique.

Flip It

OBJECT OF PLAY

Often, a change in a problem or situation comes simply from a change in our perspectives. Flip It! is a quick game designed to show players that perspectives are made, not born. We can choose to see the glass as either half full or half empty, but often when we perceive it as half full, we get better results. This game is at its best when players begin to see challenges as opportunities and to make doable suggestions around solving problems rather than just rehashing them.

NUMBER OF PLAYERS

5–20

DURATION OF PLAY

30 minutes to 1 hour

HOW TO PLAY

1. Before the meeting, hang four to eight sheets of flip-chart paper on a wall (as shown in the following figure), and on any sheet in the top row, write the name of the game.

2. On the bottom-left sheet write the word "FEAR". If you'd like, spend time drawing a representation of fear on the sheets beforehand or cut out an image from a magazine that embodies it. Tell the group that Flip It is about the future—of their department, their organization, their product/service, whatever topic you've agreed on beforehand.

3. Ask the players to quietly spend 5–10 minutes writing concerns, issues, and fears about the topic on sticky notes. Remind them to be honest about their fears because this game gives them an opportunity to reframe their fears. Collect and post the sticky notes on the FEAR sheets, which are all the sheets along the bottom row. Discuss the content with the group and ask for volunteers to elaborate on their contributions.

4. On the top-left sheet write the word "HOPE". Ask the players to survey the content in the FEAR row and try to "flip" the perspectives by reframing in terms of hope. Give them 10–15 minutes to generate sticky notes that respond to the fears.

5. With the group, collect and post the second set of sticky notes on the HOPE sheets along the top row.

6. Discuss the content with the group and ask for volunteers to elaborate on their contributions. Ask the players to dot vote next to the hopes they can take practical action on. With the group, observe the hopes that won the most votes.

7. Write the word "TRACTION" on another sheet of flip-chart paper. Rewrite (or remove and restick) the hopes that won the most votes on the TRACTION sheet. Ask the players to brainstorm aloud any actionable items related to each hope. Write them down and discuss.

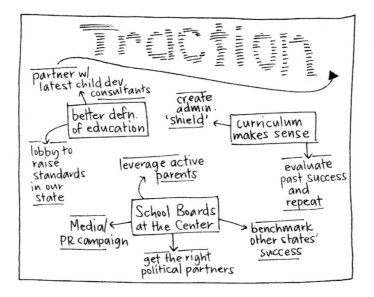

STRATEGY

Because Flip It starts with FEARS, as the meeting leader you'll need to reassure folks early on that they're not going to wallow in their fears. They just need to spend some time generating fears in order to gather information and get the game moving. You can model the flip-it behavior by opening the game with an example of a situation you chose to perceive one way or the other. Once the group writes down their fears and posts them on the wall, let them air any related thoughts and then spend the majority of the time flipping the fears into positive outcomes. You want the group to see concerns (even if it's a momentary view) as a chance to be hopeful and get motivated around action.

If you're working with a larger group or if the group generates an abundant amount of sticky notes, use the sorting and clustering technique and generate representative categories for each cluster. Then ask the group to vote on those categories and use them during the TRACTION activity. Unless directed otherwise, the issues provided by the group will likely focus on both internal and external factors. If you don't want the play to be that all-encompassing, establish a boundary going in.

Optional activity: Ask for volunteers to write their initials next to the practical actions they could support. Tell them it's not an intractable commitment, just an indication of where their interest lies.

The source of the Flip It game is unknown.

Force Field Analysis

OBJECT OF PLAY

The Greek philosopher Heraclitus asserted that change alone is unchanging. This is certainly true in today's competitive global marketplace. As employees, we're often responsible for understanding and even anticipating change in order to stay ahead. The Force Field Analysis game is a time-tested way to evaluate the forces that affect change which can ultimately affect our organizations. Making a deliberate effort to see the system surrounding change can help us steer the change in the direction we want it to move.

NUMBER OF PLAYERS

5–30

DURATION OF PLAY

30 minutes to 1.5 hours

HOW TO PLAY

1. Before the meeting, draw a picture of a potential change in the middle of a large sheet of paper or a whiteboard. You can draw a literal representation (e.g., a manufacturing plant) or a more abstract representation (e.g., a metaphor). Label the picture to ensure that everyone participating will be clear on the topic.

2. On the top left of the page, write the phrase "Forces FOR Change". On the top right, write the phrase "Forces AGAINST Change".

3. Draw arrows on both sides pointing toward the image in the middle. These will be the areas that contain categories generated by the group, so make the arrows large enough to write 1–2-inch letters inside. If you like the "wow" factor of drawing live with the group but you're not yet comfortable with freehand, sketch the arrows in pencil or yellow marker and trace them during the meeting.

4. When the group is gathered, introduce the change topic and explain that the goal of the Force Field Analysis game is to evaluate the feasibility of that change.

5. Ask the players to take 5–10 minutes and quietly generate ideas about what elements are driving the change. Tell them to include one idea per sticky note.

6. Ask the players to take 5–10 minutes and quietly generate ideas about what elements are restraining the change.

7. Draw a simple scale with a range of 1 to 5 on your main flip chart. Indicate that 1 means the force is weak and 5 means the force is strong. Ask them to review each idea FOR change and add a number to that sticky note, weighting that idea. Ask them to review each idea AGAINST change and add a number to that sticky note, weighting that idea.

8. Gather all of the sticky notes FOR change and post them to any flat surface viewable by the players.

9. With the group's collaboration, sort the ideas based on their affinity to other ideas. For example, if they produced three sticky notes that say "Can't continue production at current cost", "Materials cost too high", and "Overexpenditure on production", cluster those ideas together. Create multiple clusters until you have clustered the majority of the sticky notes. Place outliers separate from the clusters but still in playing range.

10. After the sorting activity is complete, begin a group conversation to create an overarching category for each cluster. For example, an overarching category for the cluster from step 9 might be "unsustainable costs".

11. As the group makes suggestions and finds agreement on categories, write those categories inside the arrows on the main visual.

12. As you categorize each cluster, direct the group's attention to the numeric scores within that cluster. Get an average for each cluster and write that number next to the related category in the arrow.

13. Repeat steps 8–12 using the sticky notes generated AGAINST change.

14. Add the quantities for and against change and write the totals at the bottom and on the appropriate side of the sheet.

15. Summarize the overall findings with the group, including the numeric totals, and discuss the implications of whether change should occur.

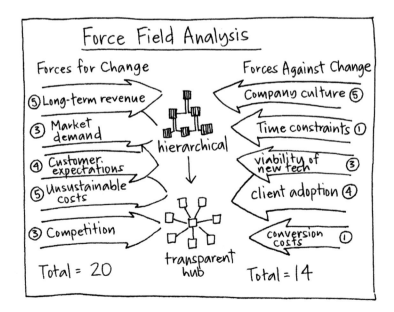

STRATEGY

Often when you play the Force Field Analysis game, it will not be the first time the players have considered the change under discussion. Many of them will have preconceived beliefs about whether the change should occur. So, be aware of group dynamics—whether they're eager for or resistant to the change. If you sense that they're eager, encourage them to give equal consideration to forces against it. If they seem reluctant, encourage them to imagine their wildest dream with respect to this change and describe what's already in place to support it. Don't let employees with fixed perspectives on either side dominate the conversation.

This game is about exploring the viability of change in an open-minded way. So, be sure to acknowledge and discuss any ideas that end up as outliers in the clusters—they frequently turn out to be valuable by offering unforeseen perspectives. Along that same line, don't assume that the numeric totals resolutely answer the question of whether change should occur. The totals are another gauge by which to measure where the group may stand. Use them as fodder for further conversation and evaluation. And if you want to take the evaluation further, ask the group to look for meta-categories after they've brainstormed the categories within the arrows. Meta-categories should be a level higher than the categories generated from the clusters. They could include "politics", "economics", "company culture", or "mid-level management". Seeing meta-categories can also help the group determine where the bulk of the evaluation may need to be focused.

This game is based on the Force Field Analysis framework developed by Kurt Lewin.

Give-and-Take Matrix

OBJECT OF PLAY

The goal of this game is to map out the motivations and interactions among actors in a system. The actors in this case may be as small-scale as individuals who need to work together to accomplish a task, or as large-scale as organizations brought together for a long-term purpose. A give-and-take matrix is a useful diagnostic tool, and helps players explore how value flows through the group.

NUMBER OF PLAYERS

Small group

DURATION OF PLAY

1 hour or more

HOW TO PLAY

To begin, you will need a list of all the actors in the system. This may be prepared in advance or generated at the start of the exercise.

Using the list, create a matrix with the list of actors along both the horizontal and vertical axes.

Each cell in the matrix captures only one direction of the flow. For example, a supplier may give a certain value to a manufacturer, but a manufacturer will give a different value to the supplier. For consistency, the vertical axis can be considered the "from" and the horizontal axis the "to."

> **Primary motivations:** For each actor in the matrix, fill in "what they want" out of the system. This information goes along the diagonal, where the individual actors intersect with themselves. These should be brief phrases that describe a goal or reason the actor participates in the system.

> **Intersecting interests:** The next step is to look at the intersections, and capture what value flows between the actors. Start with a single actor and work through each cell, asking "What can I offer you?"

For some intersection points, this will be easier to describe. In other cases, the matrix will expose previously unconnected actors and possibly those at odds with each other. The goal in completing the matrix is to find the most complete picture of how each actor can benefit all the others.

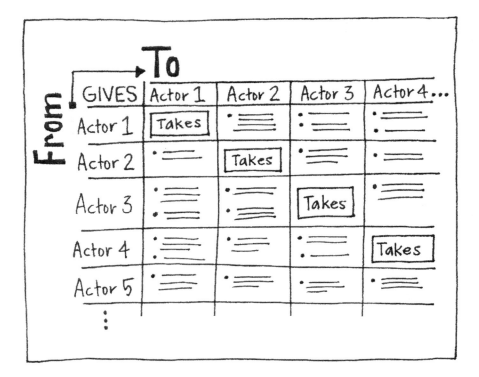

STRATEGY

Completing this matrix may involve research both before and after the initial mapping process. By using surveys or interviews, players may be able to explore and validate both the initial inputs and the intersecting interests.

Along with stakeholder analysis and boundary mapping, the Give-and-Take Matrix helps players explore and define the actors and interactions within a system.

The Give-and-Take Matrix is inspired by a number of techniques used in engineering, chemistry, and design.

Heart, Hand, Mind

OBJECT OF PLAY

The object of this game is to examine an issue from another perspective, and find significance in the issue.

NUMBER OF PLAYERS

1–10

DURATION OF PLAY

10 minutes to 1 hour

HOW TO PLAY

1. Look at an issue, product, or course of action using these three lenses:

   • Heart: What makes it emotionally engaging?

   • Hand: What makes it tangible and practical?

   • Mind: What makes it logical and sensible?

2. List the characteristics or features that appeal to each lens.

3. Score the categories from 1 to 10. Evaluate strengths and weaknesses.

STRATEGY

Significant products, activities, and experiences appeal to a whole person; they "feed the heart, hand, and mind." Use these three lenses as a means of finding, clarifying, or diagnosing the meaning of any endeavor.

The Heart, Hand, Mind game was inspired by Swiss educational reformer Heinrich Pestalozzi.

Help Me Understand

OBJECT OF PLAY

Help Me Understand is based on the underlying (and accurate) assumption is that employees come to meetings with widely different questions around a topic or a change. It assumes leadership can anticipate *some* questions and concerns but can't possibly anticipate them all. No one knows the questions employees have better than the employees themselves, so this game gives them a chance to externalize what's on their minds and have leadership be responsive in a setting outside the once-a-year leadership retreat. It also allows the players to discover overlaps with other players' questions and to notice the frequency with which those questions occur—something they may not have known prior to the meeting. It lets some sunshine in around a project, initiative, or change so that employees—who have to implement that change—have fewer lingering questions.

NUMBER OF PLAYERS

5–25

DURATION OF PLAY

30 minutes to 1.5 hours

HOW TO PLAY

1. In a large white space visible to all the players, write the topic of the meeting and the following words as headers across the top: "WHO?", "WHAT?", "WHEN?", "WHERE?", and "HOW?". Give all players access to sticky notes and markers.

2. Tell the players that the goal of the game is to let leadership understand and be responsive to any and all questions around the topic.

3. Start with the question "WHO?" and give the players five minutes to silently write down as many questions as they can that begin with the word *WHO*.

4. Ask the players to post all of their questions in the white space under WHO? and then ask for a couple of volunteers to cluster the questions according to topical similarity.

5. Bring the largest clusters to the group's attention—circle them if you prefer—and ask leadership to offer a response to the most common questions in the clusters and to any outlier questions that look interesting.

6. Repeat this process for the remaining four header questions, each time asking leadership to respond to the questions that seem the most salient to the group.

7. When the meeting closes, gather all of the questions so that leadership has the opportunity to review them later and respond to important questions that weren't covered during the meeting.

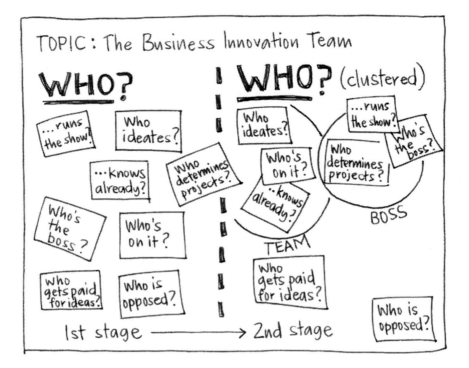

STRATEGY

As the group leader, you can conduct this game in different ways. One way is to ask the five questions back to back, with the players creating sticky notes for all five questions—WHO?, WHAT?, WHEN?, WHERE?, and HOW?—and then posting and clustering them during the first half of the meeting. After they've completed that part of the game, the players ask leadership to address the major clusters during the second half of the meeting. Another approach is to let leadership intersperse responses while the players tackle the header questions one at a time. There are benefits to both approaches.

The first approach allows the players to write questions uninterrupted by content from and reactions to leadership. It also allows leadership to save some time since they only technically need to attend the second half of the session. The second approach breaks up the flow a bit but will inevitably affect the types of questions the players ask since they're getting information from leadership as they go. Choose what's appropriate based on your knowledge of the group.

During the clustering part of the game, you may want to write emergent themes near each cluster to give leadership summaries of where their employees' attention is. This is also helpful for the players to reinforce that they have shared concerns. The themes should be one- to three-word phrases summarizing the general content of the clusters. And as the meeting leader, encourage employees to make the most of this game since it presents an unusual opportunity for them to pose real, substantive questions directly to their company leaders.

This game is an adaptation of WHO WHAT WHEN WHERE and HOW from Facilitator's Guide to Participatory Decision Making *by Sam Kaner. In his book, Kamen notes that his use of this tool was inspired by an exercise called "Five W's and H" in* Techniques of Structured Problem Solving, Second Edition, *by A. B. VanGundy, Jr., p. 46.*

Make a World

OBJECT OF PLAY

The Make a World game appeals to visual, auditory, and kinesthetic learners because of its layers of interaction. It's useful (and downright fun) because it lets players imagine the future and take action to create a first version of it. All successful ventures start with a vision and some small, initial effort toward crystallization. Alexander Graham Bell's vision for the telephone started as highly rudimentary sketches. The purpose of Make a World is to create a three-dimensional model of a desired future state.

NUMBER OF PLAYERS

8–20

DURATION OF PLAY

45 minutes to 1.5 hours

HOW TO PLAY

1. Before the meeting, determine a meeting topic. It can be any topic that would benefit from the group advancing it to a desired future state (e.g., "Our new branch location in Austin" or "Our future marketing strategy").

2. Tell the players the meeting topic and give them access to flip-chart paper, markers, sticky notes, pipe cleaners, modeling clay, magazines, index cards, tape—any art supplies available to help them "make a world."

3. Break the players into groups of three or four and give them 10–15 minutes to agree on a shared vision to make into a three-dimensional world. Explain that the world can include people, scenes, buildings, products and features, and anything they deem necessary to show an idealized version of the topic.

4. Give the players 20–30 minutes to brainstorm the attributes of the world and physically create it using art supplies.

5. When the time is up, give the players five minutes to create a slogan or tagline to summarize their world.

6. Have each group showcase their "Eden" and give the others insight into what it offers. Make note of any recurring themes or parallel features in these "fantasy lands."

STRATEGY

Any desired state can be visualized. The game isn't confined to creating 3D models of widgets or parks or products or real estate. The "world" that players create could be a new landscape for a video game, a happier and more aligned team, a globally distributed supply chain, and so forth. The challenge for each group will be in the process of ideating and creating without shutting out possibilities. Encourage them to be expansive in their thinking. In this game, players are limited only by their imaginations and their art supplies.

The title of this game was inspired by Ed Emberley's book, Make a World.

Mood Board

OBJECT OF PLAY

The object of this game is to create a poster or collage that captures the overall "feel" of an idea. The mood board may be used throughout development as a frame of reference or inspiration. It may be composed of visual or written artifacts—photos clipped from magazines, physical objects, color swatches, or anything that communicates the overall flow and feel of an idea.

NUMBER OF PLAYERS

1–10

DURATION OF PLAY

30 minutes to 2 hours

HOW TO PLAY

Although mood boards are common in design disciplines, creating a mood board does not require professional expertise. Any group that is at the beginning of a project may benefit from creating a mood board; all they need is the raw material and the idea to interpret.

Gather visual material from stacks of magazines, the Web, or even corporate presentations. Everything else—scissors, tape, blank paper, and flip charts—can be found in most office supply closets. Bring the group together around the materials and the theme that they will be interpreting. Here are some to consider:

- "Our Culture"
- "Next Year"
- "The New Product"

Small teams may co-create a single mood board from individual contributions; larger groups may interpret the theme separately and then share them with each other. It's important that every participant gets a chance to contribute elements to the board and to explain their imagery.

STRATEGY

When participants are selecting and contributing elements to a board they are best advised to do so "from the gut" and not to overly rationalize their choices. A mood board is an artifact that captures the "feel" of an idea, not a comprehensive description or a requirements document!

The game is complete when the board is complete, but the board should live on after the process. It is invaluable to keep the board visible and persistent throughout development.

Mood boards are a traditional design practice and are often a feature in the architectural practice called charette—*an intense period of collaborative group design activity around a shared goal.*

Open Space

OBJECT OF PLAY

Open Space technology is a method for hosting large events, such as retreats and conferences, without a prepared agenda. Instead, participants are brought together under a guiding purpose and create the agenda for themselves in a bulletin-board fashion. These items become potential breakout sessions, and participants have the freedom to "vote with their feet" by moving between breakouts.

Open Space was founded by Harrison Owen in the 1980s out of a desire to "open the space" for people to self-organize around a purpose. Many meetings and examples have been recorded at Openspaceworld.org. Hosting a small Open Space meeting is fairly straightforward, but requires an amount of "letting go" on the part of the organizer, who must recognize that the participants will develop a richer approach and solution to the challenge at hand.

NUMBER OF PLAYERS

5–2,000

DURATION OF PLAY

A day or longer

HOW TO PLAY

Setup: An Open Invitation

Perhaps the most important work of the organizer is developing a compelling invitation. The ideal invitation will frame a challenge that is urgent, important, and complex enough to require a diverse set of perspectives to solve.

It might sound as simple as "How can we revitalize our city's schools?" or "What's our strategic direction?"

Create the Marketplace

At the start of the process, participants sit in a circle, or in concentric circles, to get oriented and start to create their agenda. Given the challenge of the meeting, participants are invited to come to the center and write out an issue they're passionate about, and then post it on a "marketplace" wall with a time and place at which they are willing to host the discussion.

All are invited to create an item for the marketplace, but no one is required to. Creating the agenda in this fashion should take between 60 and 90 minutes.

The "Law of Two Feet"

The breakouts then begin, typically lasting 90 minutes per session. Participants may organize their breakouts however they see fit; the host records the discussion so that others may join the conversation at any time. Participants are asked to observe the one law of Open Space, the *Law of Two Feet*, which asks that if you find yourself neither learning nor contributing, use your two feet to go somewhere else. In this sense, participants are given full responsibility over their learning and contributions.

Pulling It All Together

Breakouts may last for a day or more, depending on the scope of the event. Closing the event may take many forms, the least desirable of which is a formal report from the groups. Instead, return to the circle arrangement that started the event, and open the space again for participants who want to reflect on what they've discovered and their next steps.

STRATEGY

Keep in mind the four principles of Open Space that will help set the tone of the event:

1. Whoever comes are the right people. Passion is more important than position on an org chart.

2. Whenever it starts is the right time. Spirit and creativity do not run on the clock.

3. Whatever happens is the only thing that could have. Dwelling or complaining about past events and missed opportunities is a waste of time; move on.

4. When it's over, it's over. When a conversation is finished, move on. Do the work, not the time.

Open Space game rules been popularized and incorporated into many self-organizing events which are known under different names, most prominently BarCamps and Unconferences.

The concept of Open Space was put forth in Open Space Technology: A User's Guide, *by Harrison Owen.*

Pain-Gain Map

OBJECT OF PLAY

The object of this game is to develop an understanding of motivations and decisions.

NUMBER OF PLAYERS

3–10

DURATION OF PLAY

10–15 minutes

HOW TO PLAY

Many decisions often boil down to one's basic choices between benefit and harm. By capturing these specifics for a key person, your group may uncover the most relevant points to bring up in presenting or influencing the key person's decision.

This key person may be the ultimate user of a product or may be the leader of an organization whose approval is sought.

Start by writing the key person's name or creating a quick sketch of him on a wall. Ask about this person's pains first by prompting the group to step inside his mind and think and feel as he does. Capture the answers on one side of the person:

- What does a bad day look like for him?
- What is he afraid of?
- What keeps him awake at night?
- What is he responsible for?
- What obstacles stand in his way?

A persona's gains can be the inversion of the pain situation—or can go beyond. Capture these on the opposite side by asking:

- What does this person want and aspire to?
- How does he measure success?
- Given the subject at hand, how could this person benefit?
- What can we offer this person?

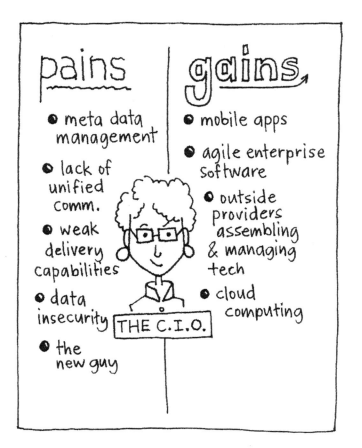

STRATEGY

Summarize and prioritize the top pains and gains from the exercise. Use them when developing presentations, value propositions, or any other instance where you are trying to influence a decision.

The Pain-Gain Map game is credited to Dave Gray.

The Pitch

OBJECT OF PLAY

It is easy to come up with concepts in a world of imagination, where money, time and technical capacity are unlimited, or to generate ideas that look good in theory, but are impractical in reality. The Pitch is a role playing game designed to bring attention back to real world and focus on feasible and viable aspects of concepts (What are the key selling points? How can this make money? Why will people buy it?). The players need to imagine that they are entrepreneurs and that need to sell their idea to a group of rich venture capitalists (VCs).

NUMBER OF PLAYERS

4–12

DURATION OF PLAY

30 minutes to 1.5 hour

HOW TO PLAY

1. Divide people into small groups, ideally pairs or triads. One group should take the role the VCs, while the others are 'entrepreneurs'.

2. A product or service is defined and agreed by the group.

3. Individually, each group spends 10 minutes formulating their pitch to be presented to the VCs. They can write, draw and rehearse: the creation is really up to each group. Ideally they should be in separate rooms or breakout spaces while creating the pitches

4. All groups should be aware that one or two representatives will present the pitch verbally to the VCs but the whole group will answer their questions. It is also important to cap preparation time (around 10 minutes is good), since over-elaborating an idea can take away the true nature of their thoughts.

5. Towards the end of the preparation time, the VCs give groups a time-warning: 'You have 2 minutes prep remaining'.

6. Each group then presents their pitch - a time limit (3 minutes) is given for each presentation and the VCs can ask up to two questions each.

7. It's not essential, but to add a sense of competition, the VCs can decide which pitch is the winner at the end.

STRATEGY

The idea behind this game is to capture the different perspectives that different groups have about a product, prototype, service or concept. Preparing a pitch to a venture capitalist obliges participants to focus on the really important ideas and the time limit helps them to concentrate on the core of the proposition. Because different groups will emphasize different aspects, it also provides a range of perspectives on the main idea being discussed. The questions the VCs ask usually expose weak points or help clarify ideas, which can then be shared and discussed by the group.

This game is also good for capturing the type of language people use to define a concept, product, service or situation, so you should encourage participants not to over-think the words they use in their pitch. If participants don't know each other, it's interesting to make a competition out of it, and even offer a prize to the winner: the shared goal of 'winning the game' usually brings teams together quickly.

The Pitch game is credited to Sarah Rink.

Product Pinocchio

OBJECT OF PLAY

Quite naturally, most of us don't think of products or services as being alive and animate. But there are a lot of benefits to imagining a product as a friend rather than an instrument. By pretending that a product has come to life, we can personalize and evolve its features in a way that is not accessible to us when we think of it as inanimate. Product Pinocchio is a game designed to establish, refine, and evolve the features of a product or service so that it becomes more valuable to the end user. By personifying it, we can better relate to it and better craft it into a "friend" that a consumer might want to take home.

NUMBER OF PLAYERS

5–20

DURATION OF PLAY

1 hour

HOW TO PLAY

1. For this game, a "scene" is any simple situation in which the character (the product or service) is required to make a decision or take action. Scene examples might be "someone attempts to steal an old lady's purse" or "a driver encounters a hitchhiker on the way to a party". Before the meeting, invent four scenes and write them on index cards, one scene per card.

2. Also before the meeting, write each of the following five questions on the tops of flip-chart paper, one question per sheet:

   - What am I like?

   - What are my values?

   - What is my community?

   - What makes me different?

   - What is my fight?

3. Starting with "What am I like?" draw a picture of the product/service in the middle of the sheet of paper with arms, legs, and a head. (This character should be used throughout the exercise, but in different poses.)

4. Ask the group to imagine that the product or service has come to life and is now a fully developed character that they know well. Ask them to call out adjectives and phrases that describe that character and write their responses around the picture.

During this step, you can also ask players who the product/service would be if it were a cartoon character or a celebrity and write down those responses as well.

5. When you have enough information to adequately describe the character, ask the players to dot vote next to the three to five adjectives that best describe the character. Circle or highlight the information that got the most votes and make a note of it with the group.

6. Move to the "What are my values?" flip chart and draw a picture of the character. Divide the group into four small groups and give each group an index card describing a scene (or work with all four scenes as one group if you have seven or less players). Ask the players to read their scene quietly and discuss in their groups what the character would say or do in that situation.

7. Bring the groups back together and give each one an opportunity to share what they agreed their character would do. Write each response down and then ask the group as a whole what the behaviors suggest about the character's underlying values. Add their responses to the flip chart.

8. Move to the "What is my community?" flip chart and draw another picture of the character in the middle of the sheet. Ask the group who the character spends her time with. What groups does she belong to? Where does she volunteer? Who needs her the most? What do her friends have in common? What are the qualities of her community? Write down the responses.

WHAT IS MY COMMUNITY?

- search-and-rescue crews
- disaster mgmt. agencies
- Concerned parents
- fire dept.
- ISD safety patrol
- police officers
- teachers

9. Move to the "What makes me different?" flip chart and draw a picture of the character in the middle of the sheet. Ask the group how this character is different from other characters in her community. What makes her stand out? What are her strengths? What could she do better? Why would someone want her on a team? Write down the responses.

10. Move to the "What is my fight?" flip chart and draw a picture of the character in the middle of the sheet. Find out the character's mission in life. What motivates her? What keeps her up at night? What does she do for people? What is she trying to prove? What obstacles are in her way? Write these responses down.

Optional activity: Ask people to toast the character as though they were at her wedding. Alternatively, ask them to give a eulogy to a competing product or service as though they were at its funeral. Or ask the players to share a true story from the character's life, something that happened to her that makes her who she is.

11. Summarize the overall findings with the group and reflect on the personality and identity of the character the group created. Discuss the implications of the character traits, values, and behaviors on the features—current or potential—of the related product or service.

STRATEGY

This game works best when the players suspend disbelief and jump into the idea that a product has a personality, a value system, and a life. For some players it will be a hard leap to make, which is why the picture you draw is important, as are the questions you ask: they both force responses as though the "it" were a "he" or "she." Be receptive even to character names suggested during the group's interactions. Calling it "Cameron" makes it easier to imagine the product or service as a person rather than an object or a process.

Encourage storytelling during this game to flesh out the character's identity based on the scenes you concocted; for example, "What would Cameron do?" Don't discourage the group from creating outlandish characters or personality traits, because the actions taken by a zany character may lead to an innovation in the way people perceive of the use of a product or service. Let the players go as far out as they want; if need be, you can move them toward consensus on a more believable character as the game closes. Just be sure to discuss with the group the parallels between the character traits they created and the benefits those traits may have on the next version of the product or service.

The source of the Product Pinocchio is unknown.

Post the Path

OBJECT OF PLAY

The object of this game is to quickly diagnose a group's level of understanding of the steps in a process.

Often, there is a sense of confusion about who does what and when. The team is using different terms to describe their process. The group has no documented process. Things seem to be happening in an ad hoc fashion, invisibly, or by chance.

Through this exercise, the group will define an existing process at a high level and uncover areas of confusion or misunderstanding. In most cases, this can flow naturally into a discussion of what to do about those unclear areas. This exercise will not generally result in a new or better process but rather a better understanding of the current one.

NUMBER OF PLAYERS

2–10

DURATION OF PLAY

30 minutes to 1 hour

HOW TO PLAY

Introduce the exercise by framing the objective: "This is a group activity, where we will create a picture of how we create [x]." X in this case is the output of the process; it may be a document, a product, an agreement, or the like. Write or draw the output of the process on the wall.

Establish a common starting point of the process with the group. This could sound like "the beginning of the day" or "the start of a quarter" or "after we finished the last one." This is the trigger or triggers that kick off the process. If you believe the group will have a hard time with this simple step, decide it for them in advance and present it as a best guess. Write this step on a sticky note, put it on the wall, and then proceed with the exercise.

1. Instruct participants to think about the process from beginning to end. Then give them the task: write down the steps in the process. They can use as many notes as they like, but each step must be a separate note.

2. After the participants have brainstormed their version of the steps, ask them to come up to the wall and post them to compare. The group should place their steps above and below one another's so that they can compare their versions of steps 1, 2, and so on.

3. Prompt the group to find points of agreement and confusion. Look for terminology problems, where participants may be using different words to describe the same step. Points of confusion may surface where "something magical happens" or no one is really clear on a step.

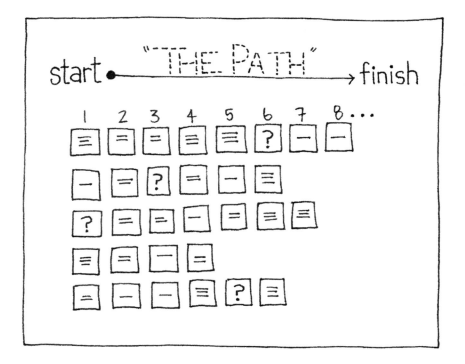

STRATEGY

The group will draw their own conclusions about what the different versions of the process mean and what they can or should do about it.

For a larger group, you may want to avoid individual readouts and instead have people post up simultaneously.

If you sense in advance that the group will get caught up in the details, ask them to produce a limited number of steps—try 10.

The Post the Path game is credited to James Macanufo.

RACI Matrix

OBJECT OF PLAY

Sometimes responsibilities aren't clear. Nothing erodes morale and performance faster than a difficult problem that belongs to someone else—or to everyone. When these situations raise their head, it may be necessary to call a group together to sort out who does what. By creating a RACI (Responsible, Accountable, Consulted, Informed) matrix, a group will tackle the responsibility problem directly.

NUMBER OF PLAYERS

2–6

DURATION OF PLAY

1.5 hours

HOW TO PLAY

To set up the matrix, you will need two lists:

A work breakdown: These are the items or activities that the group shares responsibility for creating or managing. These should be specific enough to answer when a team member asks, "Who does X?"

A list of roles: Instead of creating a list of individuals, create a list of roles that represent a group of related tasks. For example, "Project Manager", "Business Analyst", and "Architect" are better than "Tim", "Bob", and "Mary" because individuals can play multiple roles on a project, and multiple people can contribute to a single role.

R. A. C. I.
Responsible Accountable Consulted Informed

	Expert Witness	Case Manager	Consultant
provides testimony	R	A	A
prepares documents	I	A	R
project manages	I	R	C

Create the matrix by listing the work breakdown along the vertical axis and the roles along the horizontal axis. Inside the matrix, the group will work through assigning levels of responsibility by coding R, A, C, I:

Responsible: This is the *doer* of the work. Although this person may delegate or seek support from others, ultimately this one person is responsible for doing the work.

Accountable: This person is accountable for the work that the *Responsible* person does, and signs off on the work. The golden rule of RACI is that only one person can be *Accountable* for each task.

Consulted: These contributors provide input, opinions, and advice through two-way communication.

Informed: Although they are not contributors, these people are kept up-to-date on progress or completion through one-way communication.

In working through the matrix with the group, it is best to follow the natural progression of the work breakdown from start to finish. The matrix is complete when every task has a clear set of responsibilities.

STRATEGY

The work breakdown is needed to set up the matrix, but don't be reluctant to change it as the group works through the matrix. In some cases, you may discover that items are unnecessary, redundant, or poorly defined. For example, where it is difficult to assign a single *Responsible* role, it may help to split the item into two smaller, better-defined pieces. Other items will have no *Responsible* role at all, and the group may decide to eliminate them.

RACI Matrix is based on the same-named diagram traditionally employed in the management of cross-functional teams.

Red:Green Cards

OBJECT OF PLAY

Feedback is difficult to manage in large group settings. For the presenter and the audience to track with each other, they need a means to communicate their approval, disagreement, or confusion as the event progresses. Red:Green Cards provide a simple means for channeling this feedback.

NUMBER OF PLAYERS

Works well in any size group, but especially useful in large groups of 20 or more

DURATION OF PLAY

A simple Red/Green exchange takes only a moment to play—the length of time it takes to ask a question. If there is disagreement or confusion about a question, time for discussion may be required.

HOW TO PLAY

Each participant needs two cards: one red and one green. During the event, they may hold up the green card to indicate their approval or the red card to indicate their disapproval. In their simplest form, the green card means "yes" and the red card means "no."

Participants may hold up the cards to answer a specific question or they may use them simply to show how they feel about a topic at any time. For example, a presenter may ask the audience directly, "Have we covered this topic sufficiently to move on?" to get a quick understanding check. Likewise, participants may hold up their cards unprompted, nodding heads and holding up green cards in response to a topic—or holding up red cards to register an objection.

STRATEGY

Using Red/Green Cards helps solve two sticky problems in large groups: it eliminates the need for "we all agree" commentary, while surfacing participants who would otherwise fume over unheard objections. In short, it's a simple way to open a feedback loop with a large group.

Red:Green Cards was developed by Jerry Michalski. In his design, yellow and gray cards may be incorporated to represent "neutral" and "confusion."

Speedboat

OBJECT OF PLAY

Speedboat is a short and sweet way to identify what your employees or clients don't like about your product/service or what's standing in the way of a desired goal. As individuals trying to build forward momentum on products or projects, we sometimes have blind spots regarding what's stopping us. This game lets you get insight from stakeholders about what they think may be an obstacle to progress.

NUMBER OF PLAYERS

5–10

DURATION OF PLAY

30 minutes

HOW TO PLAY

1. In a white space visible to the players, draw a boat with anchors attached and name the boat after the product/service or goal under discussion. This picture is the metaphor for the activity—the boat represents the product/service or goal and the anchors represent the obstacles slowing the movement toward a desired state.

2. Write the question under discussion next to the boat. For example, "What are the features you don't like about our product?" or "What's standing in the way of progress toward this goal?"

3. Introduce Speedboat as a game designed to show what might be holding a product/service or goal back. Ask the players to review the question and then take a few minutes to think about the current features of the product/service or the current environment surrounding the goal.

4. Next, ask them to take 5–10 minutes and write the features of the product/service they don't like or any variables that are in the way on sticky notes. If you'd like, you can also ask the players to estimate how much faster the boat would go (in miles or kilometers per hour) without those "anchors" and add that to their sticky notes.

5. Once they are finished, ask them to post the sticky notes on and around the anchors in the picture. Discuss the content on each sticky note and look for observations, insights, and "*ahas*". Notice recurring themes, because they can show you where there's consensus around what's holding you back.

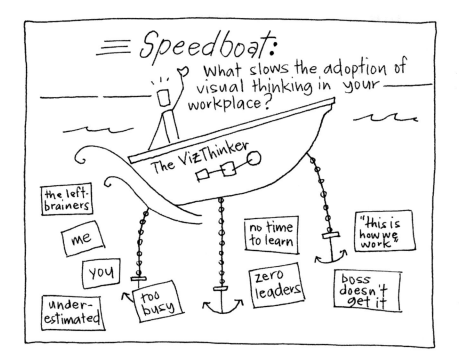

STRATEGY

This game is not about kicking off a complaint parade. It's designed to gather information about improvements or ambitions, so be careful to frame it as such. Tell the players that the intention is to reveal less-than-desirable conditions so that you can be empowered to move the product/service or goal toward an improved state.

That being said, be aware of the fact that many groups have a tendency to move immediately toward analysis of an improved state. They shift into problem-solving mode. However, doing so disrupts the nature of this game play. After the activity, it's probable that you won't have *all* the information or the right stakeholders to respond to the challenges comprehensively. So, if you hear the players critiquing or analyzing the content, gently tell them that problem solving is for another game—try to keep their attention focused solely on description, not solution.

Speedboat is based on the same-named activity in Luke Hohmann's book, Innovation Games: Creating Breakthrough Products Through Collaborative Play.

SQUID

OBJECT OF PLAY

When exploring an information space, it's important for a group to know where they are at any given time. What have we covered, and what did we leave behind? By using SQUID, a group charts out the territory as they go and can navigate accordingly.

SQUID stands for Sequential Question and Insight Diagram. It is created progressively over the course of a meeting with sticky notes, capturing questions and answers as the group moves through the space. It is flexible and will move and grow with the discussion, but it also needs to "breathe" by moving between its critical modes of questions and answers.

NUMBER OF PLAYERS

Small groups

DURATION OF PLAY

30 minutes provides optimum productivity

HOW TO PLAY

1. Reserve a large area of a whiteboard or several flip charts to create the SQUID. Participants are given two colors of sticky notes to work with, one for questions and one for answers.

2. Start to build the diagram by writing the group's core topic on a sticky note. Put this in the center of the space.

   Question mode: To open the exercise, ask individuals to generate a question that is their "best guess" on how to approach the topic. They capture this on a color-coded sticky note, and share it with the group by posting it adjacent to the center of the SQUID. The questions should immediately offer a few different routes of inquiry, and participants will likely start offering thoughts on answers.

   Answer mode: Similar to question mode, participants write their "best answers" on color-coded sticky notes. They share them with the group by posting these notes adjacent to the relevant question and connect them with a line. They may answer more than one question, and they may answer one question with multiple answers. As a rule, answers should be succinct enough to fit on one note.

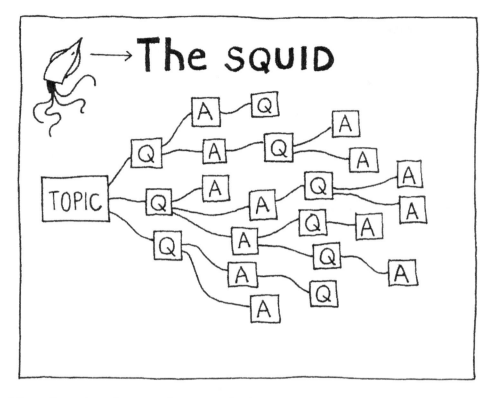

After a discussion, the group then moves back into question mode, generating questions based on the last round of answers. Participants may focus on earlier parts of the SQUID as well. The process repeats over the course of the discussion.

STRATEGY

Keeping with the current mode and not crossing questions with answers requires discipline that can only be acquired by a group through time. By working in this way, a group will train itself on the value of a systematic, rhythmic movement through unknown information, in contrast with a meandering group discussion. The SQUID itself is, of course, utterly flexible and will grow as the group directs it.

The SQUID game is credited to James Macanufo.

Staple Yourself to Something

OBJECT OF PLAY

The goal of this game is to explore or clarify a process by following an object through its flow. Through this exercise, a group will create a memorable, visual story of their core process. After it is completed, this artifact can be used to identify opportunities to improve or educate others involved in the process.

The notion of "stapling yourself to an order" comes from process improvement, but can be useful in a variety of scenarios. A group with no documented process, or an overly complex one, will benefit from the exercise. If the process is taking too long, or if no one seems to know how the work gets done, it's time to staple yourself to something and see where it goes.

NUMBER OF PLAYERS

2–10

DURATION OF PLAY

1–2 hours

HOW TO PLAY

1. The group must have an idea of what their object is, the "bouncing ball" that they will follow through the process. It's best to decide on this in advance. Some example objects could be a product, a trouble ticket, or an idea. A familiar example of this type of flow is "How a bill becomes a law."

2. Introduce the exercise by drawing the object. The goal is to focus on telling the story of this one object from point A to point B. Write these commonly understood starting and ending points on the wall.

3. Ask participants to brainstorm a list of the big steps in the process and record them on the wall. If needed, ask them to prioritize them into a desired and workable number of steps. For a high-level story, look to capture seven steps.

4. Before you start to follow the object, work out with the group the vital information you are looking to capture in the story. Ask: in each step of the process, what do we need to know? This may be the people involved, the action they're taking, or the amount of time a step takes.

5. Now it's time to draw. The group will tell the story of the object as it moves from step to step. As much as possible, capture the information visually, as though you were taking a picture of what they are describing. Some useful tools here include stick figures, arrows, and quality questions. Questions that produce an active voice in the answer, as in "Who does what here?" will be more concrete and visual. Other good questions include "What's next?" and "What's important?"

6. Be aware that the story will want to branch, loop, and link to other processes, like a river trying to break its banks. Your job is to navigate the flow with the group and keep things moving toward the end.

STRATEGY

Use the object as a focusing device. Any activity that is not directly related to the forward motion of the object can be noted and then tied off.

If possible, add a ticking clock to the story to help pace the flow. If the object needs to get to the end by a certain time, use this to your advantage by introducing it up front and referencing it as needed to keep up the momentum and interest of the story.

One trap to be aware of is that participants may move between the way things are and the way they want them to be. Be clear with the group about what state in time—today or the desired future—you are capturing.

Does the process have an owner? If someone is responsible for the process, you can use this person's expertise, but be cautious not to let her tell the entire story. This can be a learning experience for her as well, if she listens to the participants describe "their version" of the story.

There are many ways of conducting a "day in the life" type of visualization. This version of the game is credited to James Macanufo.

SWOT Analysis

OBJECT OF PLAY

In business, it can be easier to have certainty around what we want, but more difficult to understand what's impeding us in getting it. The SWOT Analysis is a long-standing technique of looking at what we have going for us with respect to a desired end state, as well as what we could improve on. It gives us an opportunity to gauge approaching opportunities and dangers, and assess the seriousness of the conditions that affect our future. When we understand those conditions, we can influence what comes next. So, if you need to evaluate your organization or team's current likelihood of success relative to an objective.

NUMBER OF PLAYERS

5–20

DURATION OF PLAY

1–2 hours

HOW TO PLAY

1. Before the meeting, write the phrase "Desired End State" and draw a picture of what it might look like on a piece of flip-chart paper.

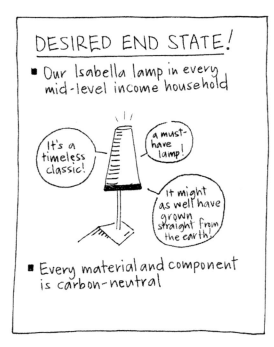

2. Create a separate four-square quadrant using four sheets of flip-chart paper. If you think the complexity of the discussion and the number of players warrants more quadrants, create as many as you'd like.

3. At the top left of the quadrant, write the word "STRENGTHS" and draw a picture depicting that concept. For example, for "STRENGTHS" you might draw a simple picture of someone holding up a car with one hand. (Yes, you're allowed to exaggerate.) Ask the players to take 5–10 minutes and quietly generate ideas about strengths they have with respect to the desired end state and write them on sticky notes, one idea per sticky note.

4. At the bottom left of the quadrant, write the word "WEAKNESSES" and draw a picture depicting that concept. Ask the players again to take 5–10 minutes to quietly generate ideas about weaknesses around the desired end state and write them on sticky notes.

5. At the top right of the quadrant, write the word "OPPORTUNITIES" and draw a picture. Ask the players to take 5–10 minutes to write ideas about opportunities on sticky notes.

6. At the bottom right of the quadrant, write the word "THREATS" and draw a picture depicting that concept. Ask the players to use this last set of 5–10 minutes to generate ideas about perceived threats and write them on sticky notes.

7. When you sense a lull in sticky-note generation, gather all of the sticky notes and post them on a flat surface that is near the quadrant and is viewable by the players. Be sure to keep the sticky notes in their original groups of strengths, weaknesses, opportunities, and threats.

8. Start with the STRENGTHS group of sticky notes and, with the players' collaboration, sort the ideas based on their affinity to other ideas. For example, if they produced three sticky notes that say "good sharing of information," "information transparency," and "people willing to share data," cluster those ideas together. Create multiple clusters until you have clustered the majority of the sticky notes. Place outliers separate from the clusters but still in playing range. (At this stage, it's important to note that if you have a group with five players or less, you can eliminate the sticky-note clustering process and simply write and draw their responses for each category as the players verbalize them. After you've gone through each section of the quadrant, players can dot vote.) Repeat the clustering and sorting process for the other categories in this order: WEAKNESSES, OPPORTUNITIES, and finally, THREATS.

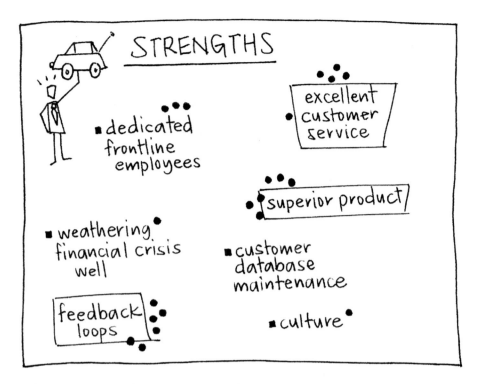

9. After the sorting and clustering is complete, start a group conversation to create a broad category for each smaller cluster. For example, a category for the cluster from step 8 might be "communication". As the group makes suggestions and finds agreement on categories, write those categories in the appropriate quadrant.

10. When the players feel comfortable with the categories, ask them to approach the quadrant and dot vote next to two or three categories in each square, indicating that they believe those to be the most relevant for that section. Circle or highlight the information that got the most votes and make a note of it with the group.

11. Summarize the overall findings in conversation with the players and ask them to discuss the implications around the desired end state.

Engage the group in a creative exercise wherein they evaluate weaknesses and threats positively, as though their presence is doing them a favor. Ask them thought-provoking questions, like "What if your competition didn't exist?" and "How does this threat have the potential to make the organization stronger?"

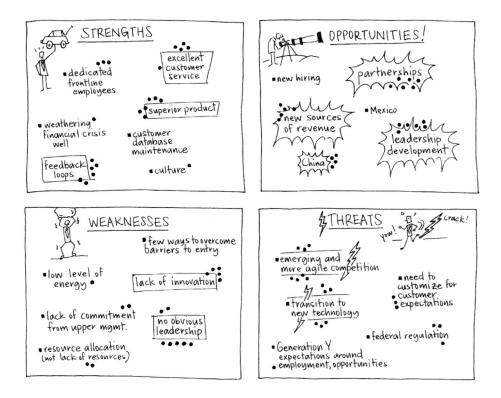

Optional activity: Lead the group in creating silly slogans for the desired end state. Let them be ridiculous: "Our lamps will light up the world." The idea is to create humor and excitement around possibilities.

STRATEGY

The SWOT Analysis is at its best when the group is unabashed in its provision and analysis of content. The players are less likely to be shy about their strengths, but they may struggle to suggest weaknesses due to sensitivity to other players or to blind spots in their own thinking. Frame the notion of "weakness" to mean something that can be improved upon. Similarly, a "threat" is something that can act as a catalyst for performance improvement. Let the group know that the higher the quality of their contributions, the better they will be able to evaluate what's on the horizon. You'll have a good sense that the game was successful when you hear the group thoughtfully consider the data and express insights they didn't have before.

This game was inspired by Albert Humphrey's traditional SWOT Analysis.

Synesthesia

OBJECT OF PLAY

By its very nature, knowledge work can be a head-heavy, deeply analytical activity. Even when the results of the work are sensory, the process of getting there is often the opposite: we think our way to solutions and filter out the five senses as irrelevant or frivolous. Through Synesthesia role play, participants examine a topic through a sensory lens, and let this inform their decisions and designs.

NUMBER OF PLAYERS

2–5

DURATION OF PLAY

15–45 minutes

HOW TO PLAY

Participants may choose to examine an existing topic or explore a new idea. It may be something as simple as "the interface for our new site" or as complex as "the user experience."

Participants choose or are randomly assigned one of the five senses: see, hear, taste, smell, and touch. Also consider including as choices temperature, position, and motion.

Participants are given a few moments to interpret a topic from the perspective of their sense and to move on to the other senses as they see fit. They then describe to the group what they perceived. For example:

- "The interface is warm to the touch. And it tastes like oranges."

- "When the app launches, it's as if I can hear an orchestra tuning up to perform. But I can't see anything; I'd like to see what they're doing."

- "The user experience stinks. It smells like a stack of dusty papers, and there is no motion. I wanted to move forward but kept getting slowed down."

STRATEGY

The Synesthesia exercise gives participants a chance to describe in visceral, memorable terms how they feel about an object or how they imagine it to be. It can uncover overlooked aspects of an idea or product or lead to new ones.

The source of the Synesthesia game is unknown.

Talking Chips

OBJECT OF PLAY

A recurring challenge in group work is managing discussions so that every individual has a chance to contribute, and no individuals dominate the meeting. By using simple "talking chips" as a currency for contribution, a group can self-manage the flow of participation.

HOW TO PLAY

1. Before the meeting starts, each participant draws a chip (poker chip, coin, or similar) from the center of the table.

2. A participant places his chip in the center to speak. Once all of the chips have been placed in the center, participants may remove their chips from the center to speak in the same manner. The process repeats.

STRATEGY

Talking chips make the value of everyone's contributions tangible and give everyone a chance to speak. They are just as effective at drawing out otherwise quiet participants as they are at containing dominant ones.

Talking chips is based on the idea of currency and was developed by Dave Gray, inspired by Byron Reeves's innovative email program, Attent.

Understanding Chain

OBJECT OF PLAY

Communicating clearly and effectively is a challenge when there is a lot to say to a lot of people. It can be tempting to try to explain "everything all at once" to an audience and fail in the process. In the Understanding Chain game, a group shifts from a content focus to an audience focus, and draws out a meaningful, linear structure for communication.

NUMBER OF PLAYERS

1–10

DURATION OF PLAY

30 minutes to 2 hours

HOW TO PLAY

To set up the game, the group needs to develop two things: an audience breakdown and a set of questions.

The audience(s): If there are a large number of audiences, break them down into meaningful groups. The groups could be as broad as "Corporate leaders" or as specific as "The guys in IT who fix the laptops." As a rule of thumb, the more specific the audience, the more tailored and effective the understanding chain will be. Each audience group will need its own understanding chain. This list of audiences could be created as a result of a WhoDo exercise (see Chapter 4).

The questions: Once the group has a clear picture of their audience, it's time to brainstorm questions. The questions frame what people really want to know and care about. Questions are best captured in the voice or thoughts of the audience, as they would ask them. They may sound like:

- "What's cool about this? Why should I care?"

- "How is this related to x, y, or z?"

- "What makes this a priority?"

Or, they may be more specific:

- "When does your technology road map converge with ours?"

- "How will it impact our product portfolio?"

The questions will become the links in the understanding chain. To generate them, the group puts itself in the mindset of the audience and captures the questions on individual sticky notes (see the Post-Up game in Chapter 4 for more information).

Play begins by sorting the questions in a horizontal line on a wall or whiteboard. This is the timeline of a communication, from beginning to end. The group may choose to:

Arrange the questions in a simple story format. In this understanding chain, the group clusters questions under three headings, from left to right:

- Situation, which sets the stage, introduces a topic and a conflict

- Complication, in which further conflict is endured and decisions are made

- Resolution, in which a course of action is chosen which leads to a result

By constructing the understanding chain as a story, the group may find the "climax"—the most critical question that leads to the resolution.

Arrange the questions in an educate-differentiate-stimulate format. In this chain, the group arranges the questions from left to right, moving from:

- Educate, in which a topic or idea and its parts are introduced

- Differentiate, in which parts of the topic are contrasted to create a basis of understanding

- Stimulate, in which actions are asked for or proposed

Arrange the questions as a conversation. In this chain, the group thinks through or role-plays a conversation with the audience and arranges the questions in an order that flows naturally. Although all conversations are different, one framework to consider is:

- Connecting: "What's up?" "What do we have in common?"

- Focusing: "What's important right now?" "What do you know about it?"

- Acting: "What should we do?"

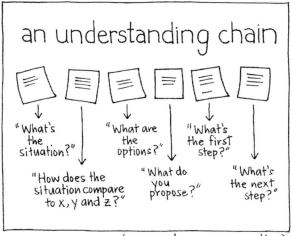

(arranged as a conversation)

STRATEGY

An understanding chain, like any chain, is only as strong as its weakest link. By examining the questions as a whole, the group may uncover an area that needs work or find the "tough questions" that are not easy to answer. A group that tackles the weak questions, and has the courage to answer the tough ones directly and honestly, will win.

The Understanding Chain game was developed by Dave Gray as part of XPLANE's consulting approach.

Value Mapping

OBJECT OF PLAY

The end goal of value mapping is to build a visual matrix that quickly and clearly defines areas of interest for something—it can be a service, a product, a plan, a website. It consists of asking people to choose a limited number of features from a bigger collection and then plotting their choices against a matrix. The result can be presented back in a template that resembles a light box, with items that were chosen more times being lit up by brighter colors and items chosen fewer times by weaker colors.

NUMBER OF PLAYERS

5–30

DURATION OF PLAY

15 minutes to 2 hours

HOW TO PLAY

This game has three main parts:

1. Define features and their groups: draw sketches or write down on cards the features or items you want participants to attribute value to. Group them in a way that makes sense to you and plot them on a table that represents these groups.

2. Play: Show the collection of feature cards to participants and have them choose a smaller number than the total, so that they must make choices and leave some features out. A good ratio is 1:3; e.g., if you have 30 cards, ask people to choose 10. Another way of doing this is to provide them with imaginary money—say, £100—and tell them they can use this budget to "shop" for features. Keep a record of each participant's choices.

3. Plotting results: Color the cards on the original table according to the number of times they were chosen. Cards that were chosen more times can be colored with stronger or brighter colors, and cards that were chosen fewer times should be colored with light colors. Cards that were never chosen should remain "uncolored." The matrix should now give you a good—and visual—idea of what areas were received with more interest, and which were not.

STRATEGY

Value mapping lets you quickly visualize things that are valued by others—consumers, members of a team, your department, your stakeholders. Understanding general areas of interest can help focus the work (where should we concentrate our efforts?) and settle internal disputes ("consumers really didn't like any of the social networking features for this application, so we don't need to invest in them now"). Try presenting the matrix in a series of slides that show different color groups—it really makes an impression!

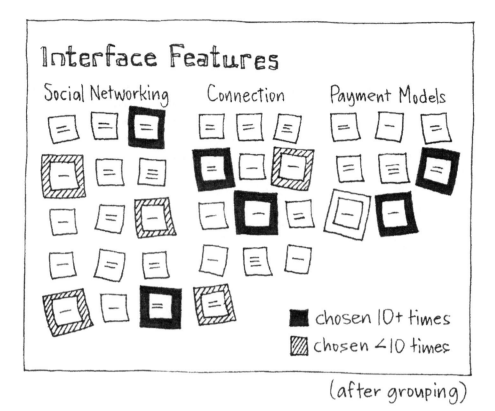

The Value Map game is credited to Sarah Rink.

The Virtuous Cycle

OBJECT OF PLAY

The goal of this game is to discover opportunities to transform an existing, linear process into a more valuable and growing process by taking a different viewpoint. This is useful in examining processes that are deemed "worth repeating," such as the customer experience.

It might be a good time to play through this exercise if the current process is transactional, compartmentalized, or wasteful. Other indications are a group that is "navelgazing" and focused primarily on its internal process, or when there is a sense that after the process is complete, no one knows what happens next.

Possible outcomes include that the group may uncover new growth and improvement opportunities in an existing process by "bending it back into itself."

NUMBER OF PLAYERS

3–10

DURATION OF PLAY

1–3 hours

HOW TO PLAY

You will need a high-level understanding or documentation of the current state of things. Any existing, linear process will work.

1. Introduce the exercise by "black boxing" the current process. This means that during the course of the exercise the group's focus will be on what's outside the process, not the fine detail of what's going on inside the box.

2. To make this visual, give each step in the process a box on the wall (medium-sized sticky notes work well) and connect them with arrows in a linear fashion.

3. To start the exercise, ask the group to think about, to the best of their knowledge, what happens before the process: Who or what is involved? What is going on? Repeat this for the end of the process: What comes after the process? What are the possible outcomes?

4. You may ask them to capture their thoughts on sticky notes and post them before and after the process.

5. Next, draw a loop from the end of the linear process back to its starting point. By doing this you are turning a linear process into a life cycle. Ask: "To get from here, and back again, what needs to happen? What's missing from the picture?"

6. The group is ready to explore possibilities and opportunities. Again, sticky notes work well for capturing ideas. Have the players capture their thoughts along the line and discuss.

Summarize or close the exercise by generating a list of questions and areas to explore. This may include looking at the internal, defined process for improvement ideas.

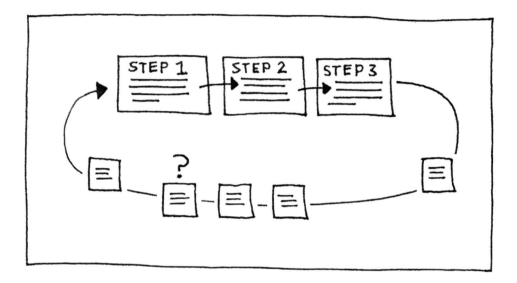

STRATEGY

Pick the right process to do this with. A process that warrants repeating, such as the customer experience, works well. Knowledge creation and capture, as well as strategic planning, are also candidates.

Get the right people in the room. Some awareness of what happens outside the process is needed, but can also hamper the experience. One of the biggest potential outcomes is a visceral change in perspective on the participants' part: from internal focus to external focus.

This game is credited to James Macanufo.

Visual Glossary

OBJECT OF PLAY

The object of this game is to clearly define a set of terms so that a group has a common vocabulary.

It's not in our nature to admit ignorance. When greeted with an unknown or abstract term, many people find it easier to pretend they understand than to ask for clarification. This is dangerous in knowledge work, where a common understanding is necessary to work together.

Groups that make time to define their terms visually will work faster and more effectively by starting on the same page.

NUMBER OF PLAYERS

2–10

DURATION OF PLAY

30 minutes to 1 hour

HOW TO PLAY

1. Introduce the exercise as a means to create a common language. The first step is to brainstorm the tough phrases and terms that make up the group's shared language. Have the group brainstorm these individually on sticky notes. Examples might be jargon, slang, technical terms, or acronyms that they use in the course of their everyday work.

2. Have participants post their notes in one large pool and examine them. Discuss which terms were the most common and which are of the highest priority for visual definition.

3. At this point, you are ready to make the glossary. From the pool, assign the most important terms a space on the wall. Pick a term to start with, and ask the group to describe it first with words. The group may uncover points that are foggy, conflicting, or inadequate in their verbiage.

4. Then try to clarify the term with a picture. Ask: what does this look like? If the term is abstract, try a diagrammatic approach. Start with the people or things involved and connect them in a way that visually captures the definition. For example, the word *social* has many definitions and contexts, but by asking the group to describe a picture of what they mean, you will get a clearer definition.

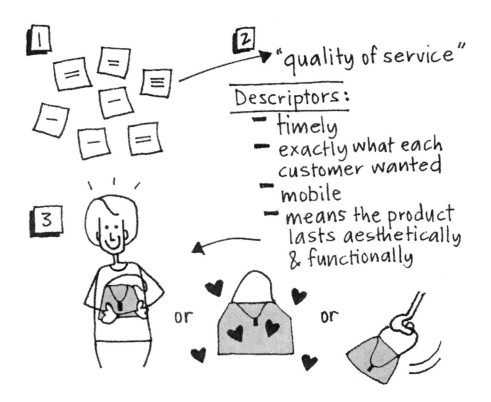

STRATEGY

Don't try to define everything up front. Find the most important terms, where there is the most opportunity to clarify, and do those first.

A good visual glossary will have utility beyond one meeting. Use the visuals in follow-on activities; make them available online, or in training materials, if appropriate. Encourage participants to use the visual elements as shorthand when communicating and working with these terms.

The Visual Glossary game is credited to James Macanufo.

Wizard of Oz

OBJECT OF PLAY

In this role-play exercise, two people prototype a machine–human interaction. The user talks to another who is "behind the curtain," playing the role of the machine. They may use a script to uncover breaking points in an existing design, or improvise to work out a completely new idea.

NUMBER OF PLAYERS

2, plus observers

DURATION OF PLAY

30 minutes or more

HOW TO PLAY

If a group is testing an existing design, they should prepare a script that outlines the responses and actions that the machine can take. The "wizard" will use this—and only this—to react to the user. For example, a group that is designing an ATM interface would write a script of information presented to the user and the responses that it understands in return.

If a group is improvising, they can just get started. To open the exercise, the two players should be visually separated from each other. This is the "curtain" that keeps them from inadvertently passing cues or other information to each other. They may be separated by a piece of cardboard, or they may simply turn their backs to each other.

The easiest way to play through the exercise is for the user to initiate some task that she wants to accomplish. As the two players play through the experience, they should look for problems, frustration points, or opportunities to do the unexpected. Essentially, the user should challenge the machine, and the machine should stick to what it knows.

STRATEGY

This technique's application has grown beyond voice control, as the "curtain" simultaneously eliminates assumptions about the machine and surfaces what the user wants to do and how she wants to do it.

The technique was pioneered in the 1970s, in the early design and testing of the now-common airport kiosk, and in IBM's development of the "listening typewriter." In these cases, the technique is taken even further: the person playing the machine would interpret voice commands from a user and manipulate a prototype of the system accordingly, like the invisible "wizard" in The Wizard of Oz.

The World Café

OBJECT OF PLAY

What's the difference between a business meeting and a conversation at a café? The World Café is a method for improving large-group discussion by borrowing concepts from the informal "café" conversations that we have all the time: round tables, cross-pollinating ideas, and pursuing questions that matter.

As a conversational process, the World Café may take on many forms. Here is a "quick-start" flow to consider, which focuses on the basics

NUMBER OF PLAYERS

24–30 participants in groups of 4–5 at round tables

DURATION OF PLAY

1.5 hours

SETUP

As the leader, you will need to find the "questions that matter" which will guide the rounds of discussion. A powerful question will be evocative and simple; it should be immediately tangible and relevant to a challenge the group faces. The group may focus on one question or move through a group of subsequent questions. For example, "How might we start having more real conversations with our customers?" may be enough to sustain three rounds of discussion.

Develop your questions that matter, and then focus on creating an inviting and hospitable environment for the event. This may not be an easy task in typical conference spaces. Some things to keep in mind include the fact that round tables are better for conversation than square tables, and each table should be equipped with drawing supplies such as markers, flip charts, and/or paper tablecloths.

HOW TO PLAY

The event consists of three 20-minute rounds of group discussion at tables, followed by a group synthesis. After each round, one person stays behind to serve as a "host" of the next round, while the rest travel to other tables as "ambassadors." In this sense, participants have a chance to go "around the world" and bring their ideas with them from table to table.

During the rounds of discussion, encourage participants to link ideas from one round to the next.

Here are some things to consider:

Spend the first few minutes talking about the last conversation. The "host" can present ideas left at the table, and the "ambassadors" should talk about what they've brought from their respective places.

Leave evidence. Draw key ideas out on the table. For the next group to appreciate the previous conversation, they will need some artifacts to respond to and build on.

Connect diverse viewpoints and respect contributions. If needed, use a "talking stick" or button to manage each other's input.

Look for patterns. By the second and third rounds, themes and larger patterns will emerge in the discussion. Encourage participants to look for these and make them evident by drawing or writing them toward the middle of the tables.

After the last round, it's time for a town hall discussion to synthesize what the groups have discovered. Referring back to the questions that matter, ask what the answers were at the different tables, and how they are connected.

A community of practitioners maintains the evolving methodology, process, history, and design principles at www.theworldcafe.com.

CHAPTER 7

Games for Closing

WE DON'T HAVE THE TIME AND RESOURCES TO DO EVERYTHING, SO WE MAKE CHOICES. Closing is the act of bringing things to conclusion, in our minds and on paper. Games that close are about finding the endpoint through prioritization, voting, and comparison, but are also about finding and creating the commitment and alignment that lead to the next step.

A good closing depends on how well a space is opened and explored. An unsatisfying set of ideas will refuse to be closed. Although closing games often define the end goal—*we need to get aligned on our five priorities*—the closing games can't do it on their own. If you are having trouble with closing, the root of your problem lies elsewhere; consider how well opened and explored the space is.

$100 Test

OBJECT OF PLAY

In this method of prioritization, participants assign relative value to a list of items by spending an imaginary $100 together. By using the concept of cash, the exercise captures more attention and keeps participants more engaged than an arbitrary point or ranking system.

NUMBER OF PLAYERS

Small groups of 3–5 participants

DURATION OF PLAY

Medium; may take up to 1.5 hours for a group to decide how to spend its money and to reflect on outcomes, depending on the length of the list and size of the group

HOW TO PLAY

To set up the game, you will need a list of items to be prioritized, set up in a matrix with space reserved for the amount spent and reasoning why.

To begin the game, explain the challenge to the group: they have a collective $100 to spend on the list of items. The dollars represent importance of items, and they must decide as a group how to allocate the dollars across the list.

Give the group sufficient time to assign their values, and ask that they also write a brief explanation for the amount. It is possible that groups may bring up the literal cost or effort of items on the list; this may confuse the primary issue of importance and it may be best addressed as a separate discussion, or as its own $100 Test.

When the matrix is complete, ask the group to explain their decisions and reasoning. The matrix can then be used as a guidepost for future decision making on a project; specifically, what items are important and of higher priority than the others.

$100 TEST

Item/Topic/Issue	$	WHY?
Internet Access	$21	to tell others & ask for help
alarm clock	$7.50	the only one often available
Telephone	$55	connect with EMS
SMS	$8.50	help during emergencies
Camera	$4.25	documentation for insurance
Solitaire	.75¢	stress relief
voice recorder	$3	capture disaster interviews

STRATEGY

This game is commonly used in software development for working with users to create their prioritized feature list. However, it can be applied in any situation where a "false scarcity" would help focus a group's wants and needs. For example, an HR group polling employees about new benefit plans may use the $100 Test to uncover what options would be best received and why.

> The $100 Test is known by many names, including Divide the Dollar and the short-form variation, the $10 Test.

The source of the $100 Test game is unknown.

20/20 Vision

OBJECT OF PLAY

The 20/20 Vision game is about getting group clarity around which projects or initiatives should be more of a priority than others. Because employees' attention is so often divided among multiple projects, it can be refreshing to refocus and realign more intently with the projects that have the biggest bang for the buck. And defining the "bang" together helps ensure that the process of prioritization is quality.

NUMBER OF PLAYERS

5–10

DURATION OF PLAY

30 minutes to 1.5 hours

HOW TO PLAY

1. Before the meeting, write any proposed project or initiative relevant to the players on sticky notes, one item per note. And when you begin, it's important that the initiatives you've written on the sticky notes are posted in random order during both stages of the game. Shuffle them before the meeting starts—you can even blind-post or ask a player to post—so that from the onset there is no implicit prioritization on your part.

2. Introduce the game by explaining to the players that 20/20 Vision is about forced prioritization based on perceived benefits. Verbalize the importance of building consensus on priorities to move the organization forward.

3. In a wall space visible to the players, post an initiative and ask the players to describe its benefits. Write their descriptions on a sticky note posted next to that initiative. If there's disagreement around the benefits of an initiative, write down both or all of the points made. Assume that there's validity to multiple perspectives and let the group indicate the majority perspective through the ranking process. If the group already has a shared sense of the benefits for each initiative, don't spend a lot of time clarifying them. Just move into prioritization and respond to questions around benefits as they organically come up.

4. Repeat step 3 for all relevant projects or initiatives until the benefits have been thoroughly described by the players, captured on sticky notes and posted.

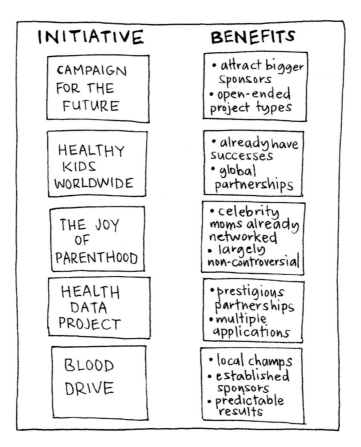

INITIATIVE	BENEFITS
CAMPAIGN FOR THE FUTURE	• attract bigger sponsors • open-ended project types
HEALTHY KIDS WORLDWIDE	• already have successes • global partnerships
THE JOY OF PARENTHOOD	• celebrity moms already networked • largely non-controversial
HEALTH DATA PROJECT	• prestigious partnerships • multiple applications
BLOOD DRIVE	• local champs • established sponsors • predictable results

5. Ask the players if any initiatives are missing from the wall. If so, request that they write them down, post them, and discuss their benefits so that you can capture them.

6. Move into a neighboring wall space, pull down two random initiatives and ask the players which they can agree are more or less important to the organization's vision or goals.

7. Post the one that the group generally agrees is more important above the one they generally agree is less important.

8. Move another initiative into the new space. Ask the players if it is more or less important than the two posted and post it accordingly—higher priorities at the top, lower priorities at the bottom.

9. Repeat this process until all initiatives have been thoroughly discussed and prioritized.

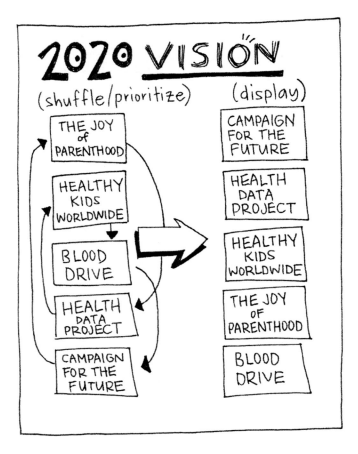

STRATEGY

20/20 Vision is about asking players to thoughtfully evaluate priorities as a group. The first phase of the game—describing and capturing the benefits—is significant because it lays the groundwork for the hard part: determining priorities. It can be challenging to get a group to rank its projects, all of which seem important in some way.

The game works best if you can facilitate general agreement around the benefits and resist the temptation to let the group waffle on prioritizing. They must make the hard decisions. And when the going gets tough, take heart: the players who resist ranking the most may also offer a wealth of insight into the initiatives and ultimately help the players better refine the final ranking.

20/20 Vision is based on and adapted from the same-named activity in Luke Hohmann's book, Innovation Games: Creating Breakthrough Products Through Collaborative Play.

Ethos, Logos, Pathos

OBJECT OF PLAY

The goal of this game is to channel Aristotle's assessment of your argument.

NUMBER OF PLAYERS

1–10

DURATION OF PLAY

10 minutes to 1 hour

HOW TO PLAY

Aristotle laid the groundwork for persuasive communication in the 4th century. Although the times have changed, effective communication hasn't. Evaluate a communication, such as a value proposition, by using the three elements of rhetoric. Role playing as your audience, score your message from 1 to 10 on these categories:

Ethos/Credibility: Who are you, and what authority do you have on the topic?

Logos/Logic: How clear and consistent is your reasoning? How do your facts measure up against my facts?

Pathos/Emotion: How vivid, memorable, and motivating is your message?

Look for areas of improvement or imbalance.

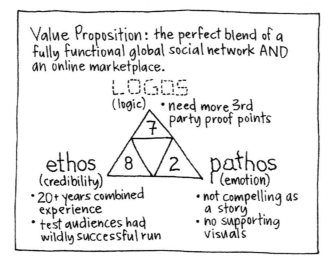

The Ethos, Logos, Pathos game is credited to James Macanufo.

Graphic Gameplan

OBJECT OF PLAY

Plenty of us are visionaries, idea generators, or, at the very least, suggestion makers. But ideas never come to fruition without a plan. As Benjamin Franklin said, "Well done is better than well said." Following up on a big idea with an executable action plan is one of the monumental differences between teams and companies that are merely good and those that are outstanding. That's why this activity deserves special attention. The Graphic Gameplan shows you how you'll get where you want to go with a project.

NUMBER OF PLAYERS

Small groups, but can also be done individually

DURATION OF PLAY

30 minutes to 2 hours

HOW TO PLAY

1. Before the meeting, think of one or more projects that need to get traction.

2. In a large, white space, preferably 3–4 feet high by 6–12 feet wide, draw a picture similar to the following.

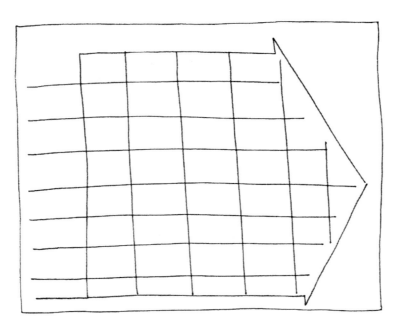

3. Display the graphic on the meeting room wall and tell the players that the goal of the meeting is to get consensus around specific tasks required to complete a project.

4. Write the name of the first project to be discussed at the top left of the first column. As the group leader, you can write all associated projects downward in that same column or you can ask the players to add projects that they agree need attention. Either way, you should end up with the relevant projects listed in the leftmost column.

5. Based on the projects listed, either tell the group the time frame and write the milestones in days, weeks, or months along the top row, or ask what they think it should be and write that time frame along the top. (Note: you can also establish a timeline after step 8.)

6. Sticky notes in hand, ask the players to choose a project and agree aloud on the first step required to accomplish it. Write their contribution on the sticky note and post it in the first box next to that project.

7. Ask the players for the second, third, and fourth steps, and so on. Keep writing their comments on sticky notes until they're satisfied that they've adequately outlined each step to complete the project.

8. Repeat steps 6 and 7 for every project on your display, until the game plan is filled out.

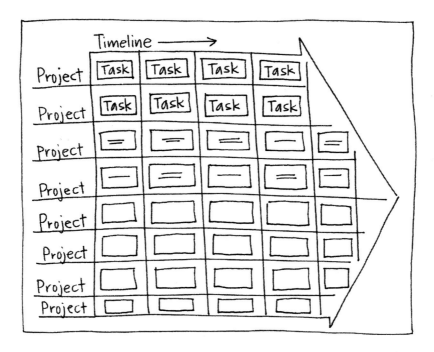

STRATEGY

Completing a game plan as a group has two major benefits. The first is that it breaks big projects into manageable chunks of work, which encourages anyone responsible for a project. The second is that because the "group mind" creates the game plan, it raises the quality of the flow of project management. It becomes less likely that important steps are left out and more likely that the project is approached thoughtfully and strategically. But as you post the sticky notes, don't assume that the first flow the group maps is the best one. Ask the players challenging questions about their comments: Does this have to happen first? Can these two steps be combined? How are steps related across projects? Do steps in one project affect the progress or outcome of another? Ask hard questions to help the group get to the best place and write any food for thought on a flip chart nearby.

When determining the timeline to write across the top, it's important to note that it can be determined *after* the project steps are established. A time frame written beforehand can impact the steps people are willing and able to take, so think about whether it serves the facilitation process better by assigning time before or after the play is complete.

If you find that the players want to assign tasks to specific people or departments as they go, let them. Simply add the names of the responsible parties to each sticky note (obviously, these assignments should be realistic). And if the players want to discuss available resources, or a lack thereof, ask them to share what they expect to need in order to complete the projects and capture that on a flip chart in the room.

The game plan can be customized with several rows and columns in order to support more complex projects. You can draw however many rows and columns you'd like as long as you have sticky notes that will fit within. Whatever the matrix looks like, the visual that results from this group discussion can serve as the large-scale, step-by-step of a project, or its contents can be funneled into more formal project management software or some other platform used by the organization. Either way, the discussion around creating it will be of significant value.

> *Optional activity: Draw smaller versions of the game plan on flip-chart paper and have breakout groups tackle specific projects using markers and small sticky notes. Then ask each group to present their approach to the larger group and to get feedback on the steps they proposed.*

The Graphic Gameplan is based on the Leader's Guide to Accompany the Graphic Gameplan Graphic Guide *from The Grove Consultants International's strategic visioning process, which involves using a template of the same name.*

Impact & Effort Matrix

OBJECT OF PLAY

In this decision-making exercise, possible actions are mapped based on two factors: effort required to implement and potential impact. Some ideas are costly, but may have a bigger long-term payoff than short-term actions. Categorizing ideas along these lines is a useful technique in decision making, as it obliges contributors to balance and evaluate suggested actions before committing to them.

NUMBER OF PLAYERS

Based on small groups, but can scale to any size

DURATION OF PLAY

30 minutes to 1 hour, depending on the size of the group

HOW TO PLAY

Given a goal, a group may have a number of ideas for how to achieve it. To open the exercise, frame the goal in terms of a "What to do" or "What we need" question. This may sound as simple as "What do we need to reach our goal?"

Ask the group to generate ideas individually on sticky notes. Then, using Post-Up, ask them to present their ideas back to the group by placing them within a 2×2 matrix that is organized by impact and effort:

> **Impact:** The potential payoff of the action
>
> **Effort:** The cost of taking the action

STRATEGY

As participants place their ideas into the matrix, the group may openly discuss the position of elements. It is not uncommon for an idea to be bolstered by the group and to move up in potential impact or down in effort. In this respect, the category of high impact, low effort will often hold the set of ideas that the group is most agreed upon and committed to.

The source of the Impact & Effort Matrix game is unknown.

Memory Wall

OBJECT OF PLAY

Employees are human beings, and every human being likes to be acknowledged. To appreciate employee contributions, celebrate their accomplishments, and build camaraderie among team members, a Memory Wall works wonders.

NUMBER OF PLAYERS

10–50

DURATION OF PLAY

45 minutes to 1.5 hours

HOW TO PLAY

1. During the meeting, give each player markers, paper, tape, and a flat surface to draw on. Make sure you have usable wall space for display purposes.

2. Ask the players to survey the other players in the room and take 10–15 minutes to write down positive, stand-out memories of working together, learning from each other, or participating in some way in organizational life.

3. Once the players have written down a few memories, ask them to draw each memory on a different sheet of letter-sized paper. Tell them they can take 20–30 minutes to draw these "memory scenes." They can partner with any person(s) involved in a memory to conjure up the details of that memory—visually or contextually.

4. When drawing time is up, ask the players to tape their scenes on the wall, forming a visual "memory cloud."

5. As the meeting leader, first ask for volunteers to approach the wall and discuss memories they posted and want to share. When you've run out of volunteers, approach memories on the wall that catch your eye and ask for the owner to share the story.

6. Summarize the experiences and ask the players to take a moment to silently recognize and appreciate those who have contributed to their work life in a positive way. Follow this game up with Happy Hour!

Optional activity: Have volunteer players approach the wall, select a memory, and try to guess who it belongs to. If they get it right, give them a door prize and ask the person whose memory it is to elaborate. If they get it wrong, open it up to the audience to guess whose memory it is. Give door prizes to multiple people if more than one gets it right.

STRATEGY

The Memory Wall isn't a game of strategy, but of appreciation. The only rule is that players should recall and draw positive, uplifting memories—nothing offensive or negative. And there is a general guideline about drawing the memory scenes: players should be discouraged from judging their drawings or the drawings of others. Tell them that the activity is designed to share anecdotes and stories—not win a drawing contest. The images are there to illustrate the scenes and, absolutely, to provide good-natured humor.

If you see a player who seems to be having trouble pulling up a memory, ask open-ended questions to bring one to the surface. And when someone has shared a memory at the memory wall, you can ask others to raise their hand if they share that memory and can offer a unique perspective. You also can make the memory wall specific to a project or milestone by drawing a large-scale visual representation of that project or milestone and asking players to recall memories related to that aspect of their work.

The source of the Memory Wall game is unknown.

NUF Test

OBJECT OF PLAY

As a group is developing ideas in a brainstorming session, it may be useful to do a quick "reality check" on proposed ideas. In the NUF Test, participants rate an idea on three criteria: to what degree is it New, Useful, and Feasible?

NUMBER OF PLAYERS

Small group

DURATION OF PLAY

Short; 15–30 minutes, depending on the size of the group and the level of discussion

HOW TO PLAY

Set up the game by quickly creating a matrix of ideas against the criteria:

New: Has the idea been tried before? An idea will score higher here if it is significantly different from approaches that have come before it. A new idea captures attention and possibility.

Useful: Does the idea actually solve the problem? An idea that solves the problem completely, without creating any new problems, will score better here.

Feasible: Can it be done? A new and useful idea still has to be weighed against its cost to implement. Ideas that require fewer resources and effort to be realized will score better here.

To play, the group rates each idea from 1 to 10 for each criterion and tallies the results. A group may choose to write down scores individually at first and then call out their results on each item and criterion to create the tally. Scoring should be done quickly, as in a "gut" check.

A discussion after the scores have been tallied may uncover uncertainties about an idea or previously underrated ideas. The group may then choose to make an idea stronger, as in "How do we make this idea more feasible with fewer resources?

	NEW	USEFUL	feasible
promotional bat·mobile	7	2	6 = 15
Facebook Group	Ø	3	10 = 13
Austin bat tours	Ø	6	8 = 14
guano fertilizer	8	9	5 = 22
sponsors for bat colonies	10	4	1 = 15

STRATEGY

The goal of this game is to check big ideas against the realities they will face after the meeting is over. It is not intended to "kill" good ideas, but to identify possible weak points so that they can be shaped and improved before seeing the light of day.

The NUF Test is an adaptation of a testing process used for patents.

Plus/Delta

OBJECT OF PLAY

The object of this game is to generate constructive feedback.

NUMBER OF PLAYERS

Any

DURATION OF PLAY

10–45 minutes

HOW TO PLAY

Make two columns: one for "plus" and one for "delta" (the Greek symbol for change).

1. Ask the group to reflect on what was positive or repeatable about an activity and capture their thoughts under the "plus" column.

2. Ask the group then to brainstorm about what they would change about it, and capture these under the "delta" column.

STRATEGY

This feedback method can apply to any activity, idea, work product, or action. By focusing on change as opposed to direct negatives, the group will be more likely to share its true assessment while also generating improvement ideas.

The source for the Plus/Delta game is unknown.

Prune the Future

OBJECT OF PLAY

People who work in large organizations know that most change doesn't happen immediately or in broad sweeps. It happens incrementally by taking small, strategic steps. Prune the Future uses a tree as a metaphor to show how the future of anything can be shaped, one leaf at a time.

NUMBER OF PLAYERS

5–15

DURATION OF PLAY

30 minutes

HOW TO PLAY

1. Before the meeting, cut a few dozen sticky notes or index cards into the shapes of leaves. Then, in a white space that will be visible to the players, draw a large tree with enough thick limbs to represent multiple categories of the future. Write the general topic under or above the tree.

2. Tell the group that the inner part of the treetop represents current states of the topic and moving outward means moving toward the future. For example, if the topic is about growing the customer base, the inner leaves would represent the current customer demographics and the outer leaves would represent future or desired customer demographics.

3. Ask the players to write current aspects of the topic—one idea per leaf—on the leaves and stick them on the inside of the treetop. Remove any redundant comments and cluster similar comments, with the group's guidance, near the appropriate branches.

4. Next, ask the players to write aspects of the future on new leaves. These can be future states or variables already in progress, or simply potentials and possibilities.

5. Tell the players to "prune" the future by posting their leaves around the treetop, related to the categories of the limbs. If you'd like, add thin or thick branches within to show relationships and let the tree grow in a natural way. If it grows asymmetrically, let that be.

6. With the players, discuss the shape of tree that emerges. Which branches have the most activity? Which areas don't seem to be experiencing growth? Where do the branches appear to be most connected? The most disconnected?

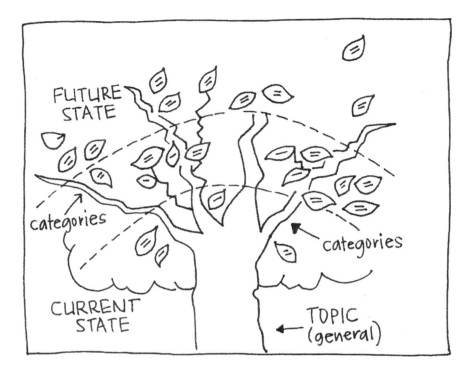

STRATEGY

The picture of the tree is the working metaphor for this game—it represents the roots of the topic, the branches of the topic, and, of course, the topic's growth potential. This game is broadly applicable because you can use a tree as a metaphor for virtually any aspect of your organization that you wish to grow or shape. The topic can be a product whose future features you want to brainstorm. It can be a team whose future roles and responsibilities you want to plan. Or you could use this game to discuss the marketplace and show where the players think it is changing or growing.

When the players start to shape the outer treetop, encourage them to "go out on a limb" with their ideas for the future. This game is about possibilities—realistic and otherwise. And if someone requests fruit on the tree to represent ROI, draw apples where they should be. If the players request another tree (or even a grove!), draw quick rudimentary trees and let the players start adding leaves, following the original procedure. This game works well because it allows for a nonlinear, organic representation of what is likely a complex topic. It results in a visual display of the interconnectedness of future conditions; showing where some parts of the tree may be suffering while others are thriving.

The Prune the Future game is based on the Prune the Product Tree activity in Luke Hohmann's book, Innovation Games: Creating Breakthrough Products Through Collaborative Play.

Start, Stop, Continue

OBJECT OF PLAY

The object of Start, Stop, Continue is to examine aspects of a situation or develop next steps.

NUMBER OF PLAYERS

1–10

DURATION OF PLAY

10 minutes to 1 hour

HOW TO PLAY

Ask the group to consider the current situation or goal and individually brainstorm actions in these three categories:

Start: What are things that we need to START doing?

Stop: What are we currently doing that we can or should STOP?

Continue: What are we doing now that works and should CONTINUE?

Have individuals share their results.

STRATEGY

This exercise is broad enough to work well as an opening or closing exercise. It's useful in framing discussion at "problem-solving" meetings, or as a way to brainstorm aspirational steps toward a vision.

The source for the Start, Stop, Continue game is unknown.

Who/What/When Matrix

OBJECT OF PLAY

It's common for people to attend meetings, voice strong opinions, and then waffle and dodge responsibility for follow-up actions. We have all been guilty of this at one point or another; it's a built-in, easy assumption that the person who called the meeting bears the responsibilities coming out of it. We may do this for a number of reasons: we don't have time to commit, we don't believe in the purpose (or people) involved, or there is no clear direction on what needs to be done next.

Many meetings end with a "next steps" or "action items" discussion. These discussions are often abstract, starting with a list of tasks that are then handed out to possibly un-willing participants with no particular deadline attached. By focusing the discussion on a Who/What/When matrix, you can connect people with clear actions they have defined and have committed to.

NUMBER OF PLAYERS

1–10

DURATION OF PLAY

15–30 minutes

HOW TO PLAY

On a flip chart or whiteboard, create a matrix that outlines WHO / WHAT / WHEN.

Although instincts may be to start with the "WHAT" (the tasks and items that need to be done), this approach starts with the "WHO" (the people who will be taking the actions). Put every participant's name into the matrix in this column.

Ask each participant what concrete next steps they can commit to. Place this in the WHAT column. Each participant may have a number of next steps that he thinks are required or feels strongly about. For each item, ask that person "WHEN" he will have the item done.

Actions don't take themselves, and people don't commit as strongly to actions as they do to each other. By approaching next steps "people-first," a few things change. First, it becomes clear that the people in the room are the ones who are accountable for next steps. Second, by making commitments in front of their peers, participants stake their credibility on taking action, and are more likely to follow through. And third, it becomes clear WHO is going to do WHAT by WHEN—and who has volunteered little or no commitment.

NEXT STEPS

WHO☺	WHAT⊡	WHEN
Bunko		5/10
Morelli		Friday
Chung		1/07
Macanufo		Mon. 9am
Brown		NOW!!
Gray		Friday

STRATEGY

In completing the Who/What/When matrix, you are likely to find that there is a lot to do. This is a good time to ask if there is any way for participants who have committed to little or nothing to step up their contribution. They may be able to assist others in completing their tasks—or their attendance may have been unnecessary.

Although participants are more likely to commit to actions they declare in front of the group, ultimately you are accountable for following up with them after the meeting. You may ask participants to email you their commitments, and you may send the group the full list as an update.

The source for Who/What/When Matrix game is unknown.

CHAPTER 8

Putting Gamestorming to Work

WE'VE TALKED ABOUT GAMES AS MICRO-WORLDS that you can create and explore to develop deeper understanding and insights about any topic. Now let's take a look at a real-life example of how a small group used gamestorming to consider solutions to a specific problem.

Imagine a World: The Betacup Story

In the summer of 2009, a group of designers met at a remote conference center to exchange ideas and practices with people from other disciplines, in an annual gathering of minds that has come to be known as Overlap.

What is Overlap? New technologies and devices are changing the way people interact with information, and designers know they need to keep up. In a world where your phone can also be your Internet browser, your TV, your music player, and your GPS device, it's no longer possible to design objects and interfaces without thinking about the complex webs of interactions they make possible. Because of this increasing complexity, design is changing from a solo activity to a team event, and designers know that the overlaps and intersections with other disciplines are where they will find the best ideas and opportunities for growth. So, they have developed an event whose entire purpose is to cross-pollinate ideas between design and other disciplines.

One of the challenges in planning an event like this is deciding how to organize the time. Every discipline has its own language, its own culture, a way of doing things. How do you bring them all together for a meaningful conversation? Do you seat everyone in a circle and talk? Do you set a topic, or ask questions, or what? At this meeting in 2009, the three authors of this book—all of us participants in the event—decided to use gamestorming as a method for managing the conversations.

So, now that you can, I think, imagine the world—a remote conference center; 50 curious, intelligent people; a desire for conversation and new ideas—I'd like to tell the story of Toby Daniels, a participant in Overlap: why he came, what happened over the weekend, and what he came away with, and how gamestorming played a role in the process.

"Be the change you want to see in the world," said Ghandi, and that's exactly what Toby Daniels had in mind when he came to Overlap that summer.

Toby is not a designer. He's a community organizer who's working to change the world. He helped to raise more than $250,000 for *charity: water*, a group working to bring clean and safe drinking water to people in developing nations. He's a board member for Camp Interactive, a nonprofit organization that empowers inner-city youth through the inspiration of the outdoors and the creative power of technology. And in the summer of 2009, Toby had identified a new project he wanted to work on.

"When I came to Overlap I had two things: a name and a well-defined business problem," he says. "I left with not only a solution, but a whole new way of thinking about the problem."

Toby's well-defined business problem was simply this: why don't more people use reusable coffee cups? Twenty million trees are cut down, and 58 billion paper cups are thrown away every year, because reusable cups are just too much hassle for most people. But Toby's big idea was that, rather than harp on people to try to get them to change their behavior he would get designers to make a better cup. The name Toby gave to his project was Betacup.

Imagine a world. Imagination begins with a question.

The world Toby wanted to imagine and explore was a world where people's coffee consumption didn't kill trees and add nonrecyclable paper cups to the world's ever-growing landfills. His question: what might that world look like?

He came to the event at the urging of a friend, who thought that the confluence of designers at Overlap might give Toby's project a much-needed boost.

"Not coming from a design background, with the idea that I would be spending three days with designers, well, I thought they would see me as a complete alien" he says. "I came with a very open mind, but thinking that I was going to be more of a passive observer. I thought I would probably be in the background, observing and trying to learn by watching."

But Toby soon realized that gamestorming changed the dynamic, involving everyone in ways that make it difficult not to participate. What follows is a brief description of four games and how they helped Toby move from problem to solution.

Game 1: Poster Session

One of the first games was an infographic Poster Session (which you read about in Chapter 5), where each player was asked to create a visual infographic, in the form of a poster, proposing a topic they would like to explore.

"This was my first opportunity to share and articulate what the Betacup was. I found the exercise initially fascinating," says Toby, "and I felt challenged and encouraged by the opportunity. It forced me to think about my project in a visual way. I started using symbols and pictures and looking to find connections. It was a good way for me to understand what I would need in order to explain it to other people."

Part of the exercise was a "gallery walk" where all the participants walked around the room to look at each other's posters. This meant the posters could not be simply visual aids for a presenter, like a PowerPoint slide. Rather, each poster needed to be standalone and self-explanatory, like an information graphic in a newspaper.

"The most challenging thing about the exercise was putting it up and having to walk away. I had to let people look at it and make their own interpretations of it. That really forced me to make my picture as clear and explanatory as possible."

The group then used a selection method called Dot Voting (which you read about in Chapter 7) to narrow the field of 50 posters down to five compelling proposals for deeper focus. Toby's was one of the five posters selected, which meant he would get the chance to present his proposal to the larger group.

"As soon as I realized I had a chance to publicly share this I got very excited. I knew that if I was given an opportunity to talk about it, combined with some kind of visual representation, that people would be interested and that I would be able to engage them," says Toby. "Each of us had about 30 seconds to pitch our idea and then people had an opportunity to 'Vote with their feet.' (See Open Space, Chapter 6.) That was definitely a scary exercise. But it was scary in a fun way. We were all able to see where the energy was, where people wanted to invest their time and effort. Happily, the Betacup drew a small crowd and we took off from there."

Game 2: Go for a Walk

Although not a formal game, whether it's a walk in the park or an informal lunch, unstructured time allows any team to gel as a unit so that all the players can get to know each other. After the poster session concluded and everyone had loosely tied themselves to one of five "project teams," the teams were invited to take a walk, get to know each other, and begin to frame out the work they wanted to do.

"The walk gave me a chance to meet the other people who had shown an interest, explore ideas with them, and think about how we wanted to take the concept forward," says Toby.

"When we were walking I decided to take a little bit of a lead in orchestrating the conversation. I didn't want to take on a leader role, but I really wanted to explore their personal experiences and how they saw the issue. Everybody who drinks coffee is complicit in some way in this problem, so we had a lot to work with.

"So I started very broadly, to get people talking about coffee experiences—everybody has experiences that relate—and then tried to narrow it down towards 'what do you want to do about this?'"

"As we were walking, everyone wanted to participate in the conversation, so the group had to reposition itself. Half the group started walking backwards. It created a new, dynamic form of interaction that lent itself to a great conversation. As we were walking, people were constantly moving and changing positions and adjusting. People broke off into splinter groups and came back. It was just so loose and unstructured and playful.

"It was surprising how much we got out of a 45-minute walk, in terms of the ideas and creativity and camaraderie that came out of that process."

Game 3: Make Something Tangible

One of the next games involved making a prototype—taking an aspect of the design challenge and making a tangible model that people could interact with in a physical way. Toby's team chose to prototype an online survey using sticky notes.

"One of the ideas that came out of our walk was to do a coffee-consumption survey, so as soon as we had the opportunity to make something we began writing out survey questions. We set about trying to really understand the coffee consumption experience and process.

"We wrote the survey questions on big sticky notes. We had something like 20 questions, and each question was on a sticky on the wall, so we could move the questions around, change the order, and dump questions, change them, or replace them if they didn't work.

"Then we got three people from outside our group to come in and do the survey in a physical way. We had each person read the questions, and then we had them write an answer on a smaller sticky note and attach the answer to the question.

"I had never designed a survey, or any other document that I think of as being screen-based, in that way. It was incredibly useful. Watching people work through a survey in that way, you can see when they are confused or don't understand a question. It's much easier to get and give feedback since you're standing right next to them, and they can say, 'Oh, I didn't understand what that means,' and so on."

Game 4: Bodystorming

Bodystorming (which you read about in Chapter 6) is a game in which players translate ideas into physical experiences which they can explore through improvisation and role playing. Using props, paper, and whatever else is handy, participants create a rough stage set that they then use to physically interact and act out ideas.

When it was time to present their ideas back to the larger group, Toby's Betacup team decided that bodystorming would be a good way for them to understand consumer coffee-buying behaviors. They re-created a Starbucks coffee house using folding chairs, paper cups, and a table, assigned people roles, and began to play out various scenarios.

"We had started the weekend thinking about the problem as a product issue, but after playing some of these knowledge games, we realized that this problem had many dimensions, which included not just the product, but also the business system and the way that consumers interacted with it," says Toby.

"We needed to work through product issues, system issues, and consumer behavior, and this was the best way for us to put all the pieces together. We needed to understand the system as a consumer, but also wanted to see it as a store manager would. Once we had set the stage, we could act out a bunch of different scenarios. Bodystorming made the whole experience fun and interactive, and it was also one of the most useful things we did.

"The brief was to explain our solution to the larger group, but we were going so strong, and had such great energy, that we decided we would just continue to explore our ideas in the hope that others could interpret what was going on," he adds. "We gave the audience a 'pause button' so they could pause the action to ask questions and so on."

The solution Toby's team found through gamestorming was not a just a better reusable cup. It was a better system. Their big idea was to digitally enable the reusable cup so that it would remember its owners' favorite drinks, could serve as a credit or debit card, and could work as a loyalty card, all in a single object. What they presented back to the larger group in their bodystorm was a Starbucks with a regular lane, like you find in today's Starbucks, and an express lane, where people with Betacups could quickly and easily order by scanning their cup, avoiding the longer "slow-serve" line. They acted out several scenarios that highlighted benefits of the Betacup. For example, someone making an office coffee run would not have to remember everyone's drink orders because that information was embedded in co-workers' Betacups. The team's solution had benefits for everyone: consumers could get their orders served faster and more accurately, and Starbucks got to serve more customers and make more money.

Gamestorming Results

The weekend came to a close, and Toby made his way back to New York. Imagine his surprise a week later, when he got a call from Jim Hanna, Starbucks' director of Environmental Affairs.

"The funny thing is that he was already on our radar as someone we wanted to talk to," says Toby. "Before I came to Overlap, I had asked one of my advisors if she knew anyone at Starbucks, and she said that I should speak to Jim Hanna, that he is definitely the main man there when it comes to looking at their environmental impact.

"Then Overlap happened and one of our team members, Brynn Evans, had written this wonderful recap of the event on her blog, and that got picked up and shared a bunch of times, and the story of what we did kind of rippled out over the Internet. Someone saw it and forwarded it to Jim and his colleagues.

"So, to get a call from Jim was a very exciting thing. I mean, everyone wants to get a meeting with Starbucks, and here they were calling us!"

The funny thing, according to Toby, is that Starbucks would not have called if Toby had pursued his original plan, which was to design a better reusable cup. There are hundreds, if not thousands, of great ideas for better disposable cups, and Starbucks is inundated with cup ideas. There is no shortage of cup ideas out there, and there's a long line of people waiting to talk to Starbucks about their better cup. But Starbucks was interested in Toby's Betacup project because it involved a community of people working together to rethink not just the cup, but also the system around the cup.

What resonated with them was the design approach that involved participation from a community, that ideas could come from anywhere and be anything, that even at the inception of the design process, a movement was already beginning to build.

"If we had talked to them earlier, before we had engaged the community, we wouldn't have gained that insight from the most important and valuable potential partner and distributor there is," says Toby. "Starbucks is definitely now one of the major supporters of what we are doing."

Starbucks now sponsors a $20,000 Betacup design challenge where hundreds of ideas have already been submitted to be voted on by the Betacup community and a panel of judges.

This is just one success story. We hope you will get out there and make your own, and share them with us for future editions of this book. By gamestorming, you can turn your ideas into action faster, better, and more cost-effectively than any other method we know of.

You can find us on the Web at *http://gogamestorm.com*. Now stop reading this book, get out there and gamestorm!

Index

Acknowledgments

Thanks are due to so many: Richard Saul Wurman for his inspiration and encouragement; David Sibbet, Alex Osterwalder, Chris Messina, and Luke Hohmann for their pioneering work, and for the design of some amazing games, and for agreeing to share them in this book; Nancy Duarte, Garr Reynolds, and Dan Roam for setting an example for us all to follow; Aric Wood, for believing in the project and many conversations along the way; Bob Logan, Alex Wright, and Jo Guldi for their help, deep knowledge, and scholarship; Michael Dila and Robin Uchida for demonstrating innovation by example; Richard Black, Lee Weldon, Louis Kim, and Stuart Curley for their assistance in the long development of the concepts, Karl Gude for just being himself; Colleen Wheeler for thoughtful and considerate editing, and for the countless hours herding cats and keeping the project on track; Brynn Evans, Toby Daniels, Marcel Botha, and all the other Overlappers for helping to test the viability and for their inspiring work on the Betacup; Liz Danzico, Andy Budd, Peter Merholz, Bill DeRouchey, and Lenore Richards for helping get *Gamestorming* off the ground; the entire UX community, which helped to guide the project through its early stages; Tim O'Reilly for making all of this possible; Edie Freedman for design leadership and shepherding the project through the design process; Isaac Milla and Alyssa Beavers for their patient understanding during the long hours it took to get the project completed; and most of all, thank you to Michelle Milla, my support, my love, my companion through thick and thin.

—Dave Gray

I typically like to take personal credit for my successes, but in most cases that's just delusion. The truth is that all of life—success, failure, triumph, and sorrow—is intricately linked to the people around us. I thank them not only for their love and (often undeserving) support, but also for the hard lessons they've taught me over the years. So these acknowledgements are to my people, in no particular order. Rocky: You are, hands down, the most awesome brother on the planet. I am so thankful for the experiences we've had together. I love you and I wouldn't be half the person I am today without you. Joe: Thank you for taking on three children when it must have felt like adopting barnyard animals. I love you and am so impressed by your fortitude and your ability to remember the punchline to every joke. "I'm glad you got to see me." Christy: I know no one with your compassion and your strength. I love you with all of my heart and I am so thankful that I can have many more years as your little sister. Cassie: You are the twinkle in everyone's eye. Thank you for your heart of gold, your incredible talents, and for thinking that Aunt Sunni is so cool. I'll be with you every step of the way through life's journey. I love you to pieces. Shannon: Guess what? Gorgeous blondes with mermaid-like hair are BADASS. Thank you for reminding me to stop making things black and white and start paying attention to the beauty and possibility in the world. Chet: You are so patient with me; I've grown light years just by being with you. I thank you for the love, the enlightenment, and the sex. Now please try to actually absorb that compliment. Aunt Marilyn: You are amazing. You continue to learn and grow and to share your wisdom with me. I love you and I thank my lucky stars that you are my aunt. Fran: Your son is amazing—nice work. Thank you for him and also for the invaluable lesson that I can enjoy life as long as I choose to. Marilyn Martin: I made it through the first few months of my entrepreneurial venture because you took a chance on me. I will always be thankful. David Sibbet: You were among the first to put visual thinking in the workplace. Thank you, too, for taking a chance on a total stranger and for giving me an opportunity to make a career out of something I love. And to all of the visual practitioners in the world. You're ahead of your time and your work is a source of constant inspiration. Long live the visual thinking revolution!

—Sunni Brown

I owe an immeasurable debt to my clients and coworkers at XPLANE, who pioneer these techniques in the real world while playing with live ammunition. This book is as much about them as for them. I'm continually grateful for their courage and enthusiasm in charting out new and uncertain territory. The techniques here are a snapshot of living, often informal, knowledge in use at any given whiteboard at any given moment around the world. In that sense, creating this book would not have been possible without the candid and open collaboration of a community of practitioners, who have helped point us to original sources, compiled research, and contributed their own games to the mix. In every case we have done our best to give credit where it is due, and I apologize in advance if we have not explicitly recognized someone's contribution. In particular, thanks to Luke Hohmann, author of *Innovation Games*, whose coaching and expertise has been invaluable. And to Scott Matthews of XPLANE, whose original "big head" doodle would become the first empathy map. I may be most indebted to my wife, Elizabeth, who continues to indulge my sense of amusement on most things and whose key value-add in this engagement included managing the scope of consultant jargon in my deliverables. Thanks for that.

—James Macanufo

About the Authors

Dave Gray is the founder and chairman of XPLANE, the visual thinking company. Founded in 1993, XPLANE has grown to be the world's leading consulting and design firm, focused on information-driven communications. Dave's time is spent researching and writing on visual business, as well as speaking, coaching, and delivering workshops to educators, corporate clients, and the public.

Dave is also a founding member of VizThink, an international community of Visual Thinkers.

Sunni Brown, M.P.A., is owner of BrightSpot Info Design, a company specializing in visual thinking to support organizational and group success. Sunni was trained in graphic facilitation at The Grove Consultants International, a San Francisco–based company that pioneered the use of visuals in meetings and group processes. She is currently an associate of The Grove, a freelance consultant for XPlane (the visual thinking company), and an associate of Alphachimp Studios. She is also cofounder of VizThink Austin, currently the largest visual thinking community in the United States.

Sunni presents regularly on the topics of graphic facilitation, graphic recording, and visual thinking. She is also a contributing researcher for Nancy Duarte's upcoming book on storytelling and presentations. Sunni holds bachelor's degrees in journalism and linguistics and a master's in public affairs from the Lyndon Baines Johnson School of Public Affairs. She lives in Austin, Texas.

As a consultant at XPLANE, **James Macanufo** helps large technology and government clients develop their vision, strategy, and communication plans. He is actively obsessed with understanding what things are, the way they work, and why they matter. He is also an active gamer and occasional inventor of card games.

Colophon

The cover, heading, and body font is Minion Pro; the game subheading font is Helvetica Neue.

Get even more for your money.

Join the O'Reilly Community, and register the O'Reilly books you own.It's free, and you'll get:

- 40% upgrade offer on O'Reilly books
- Membership discounts on books and events
- Free lifetime updates to electronic formats of books
- Multiple ebook formats, DRM FREE
- Participation in the O'Reilly community
- Newsletters
- Account management
- 100% Satisfaction Guarantee

Signing up is easy:

1. **Go to: oreilly.com/go/register**
2. **Create an O'Reilly login.**
3. **Provide your address.**
4. **Register your books.**

Note: English-language books only

To order books online:
oreilly.com/order_new

For questions about products or an order:
orders@oreilly.com

To sign up to get topic-specific email announcements and/or news about upcoming books, conferences, special offers, and new technologies:
elists@oreilly.com

For technical questions about book content:
booktech@oreilly.com

To submit new book proposals to our editors:
proposals@oreilly.com

Many O'Reilly books are available in PDF and several ebook formats. For more information:
oreilly.com/ebooks

O'REILLY®

Spreading the knowledge of innovators   www.oreilly.com

Buy this book and get access to the online edition for 45 days—for free!

Gamestorming
By Dave Gray, Sunni Brown & James Macanufo
July 2010, $29.99
ISBN 9780596804176

With Safari Books Online, you can:

Access the contents of thousands of technology and business books

- Quickly search over 7000 books and certification guides
- Download whole books or chapters in PDF format, at no extra cost, to print or read on the go
- Copy and paste code
- Save up to 35% on O'Reilly print books
- **New!** Access mobile-friendly books directly from cell phones and mobile devices

Stay up-to-date on emerging topics before the books are published

- Get on-demand access to evolving manuscripts.
- Interact directly with authors of upcoming books

Explore thousands of hours of video on technology and design topics

- Learn from expert video tutorials
- Watch and replay recorded conference sessions

To try out Safari and the online edition of this book FREE for 45 days,
go to **www.oreilly.com/go/safarienabled** and enter the coupon code HPUPGBI.
To see the complete Safari Library, visit safari.oreilly.com.

Spreading the knowledge of innovators   safari.oreilly.com

CPSIA information can be obtained at www.ICGtesting.com
Printed in the USA
267195BV00002B/105-206/P

Advance Praise for *Gamestorming*

"Gamestorming will revolutionize how you generate ideas and align your team. Moving away from brainstorming and toward gamestorming will produce outcomes unimagined."

—Nancy Duarte, CEO Duarte Design,
Author of *Slide:ology* and *Resonate*

"Wow, this IS the definitive guide to workshop methods for managers and professionals."

—Dr. Martin Eppler
Director of the Institute for Media and Communication Management
University of St.Gallen, Switzerland

"Dave, Sunni, and James weren't fooling around when they wrote Gamestorming. *It's a brilliant book that'll help every team plow through the wicked challenges they face on a daily basis, in a creative and fun way."*

—Jared M. Spool
Founding Principal of User Interface Engineering

"Life is full of games—if you want to win and have fun doing it, this is the place to start"

—Scott Berkun
Author of *Confessions of a Public Speaker*
and *The Myths of Innovation*

"At Zappos, one of our core values is to 'Be Creative, Adventurous, and Open-Minded.' Gamestorming *is a great how-to manual for achieving that."*

—Tony Hsieh
Author of *New York Times* #1 bestseller *Delivering Happiness*
and CEO of Zappos.com, Inc.